MYSPACE®, MYKIDS
Copyright © 2007 by Jason Illian
Published by Harvest House Publishers
Eugene, Oregon 97402
www.harvesthousepublishers.com

Library of Congress Cataloging-in-Publication Data

Illian, Jason.
  MySpace, MyKids / Jason Illian.
    p. cm.
  Includes bibliographical references.
  ISBN-13: 978-0-7369-2044-5 (pbk.)
  ISBN-10: 0-7369-2044-7
  1. Internet and teenagers. 2. Internet and children. 3. Online social networks. 4. Myspace.com.
I. Title. II. Title: My space and My kids.
  HQ799.2.I5.I45 2007
  305.2350285'4678—dc22
                                                                2006031307

Contents

⟨⟨⟨ ⟩⟩⟩

Part I: Perspective

1 **aWholeNewWorld.com:**
   Does God Want to Be in My Space? 7

2 **Friends and Fiends:**
   The Thin Line Between Schoolmates and Strangers 15

3 **My House Is Not a Democracy:**
   Virtual Parents and Virtual Tyrants 27

Part II: Priorities

4 **Sherlock Homes:**
   Tracking the Virtual Footprints 39

5 **Souls Without Soles:**
   Teaching Our Children Not to Leave Footprints 73

6 **My Life as a 16-Year-Old:**
   A Behind-the-Scenes Look at the Life of an Online Teenager 85

Part III: Plan

7 **Frequently Asked Questions:**
   A Quick Reference Guide to Understanding My Space 103

8 **To Protect and Connect:**
   Every Parent's Dream 113

   Notes 117

PART I:

Perspective

aWholeNewWorld.com

Does God Want to Be in MySpace?

Behold, children are a gift of the LORD,
The fruit of the womb is a reward.
Like arrows in the hand of a warrior,
So are the children of one's youth.
How blessed is the man whose quiver is full of them;
They shall not be ashamed
When they speak with their enemies in the gate.

PSALM 127:3-5 NASB

"I WANNA BE THE GIRL WHO STEALS YOUR BREATH AWAY" is a 15-year-old from Temple, Texas. When you first log onto her site, you hear the song "Vulnerable" by Secondhand Serenade. Quite appropriate, I think, because most teenagers feel just that—vulnerable.

As you surf her site, you see that she is a cheerleader and a Capricorn, and her income is over $250,000 (not sure about that last one). She also states that she is a Christian. A few sentences later, however, she begins cursing like a drunken sailor. Apparently, she is also confused. She has hundreds of friends, plenty of pictures, and personal information about her high school, the boy she likes, her brother Nick, and her eclectic musical interests.

From her site, you can link to a number of different friends, strangers, posers, dreamers, and geeks. One profile linked to her site features an 18-year-old guy playing a guitar in the buff. Another profile is of a teenage girl whose tagline is, "Even Cinderella has nightmares." A fellow classmate's profile has a survey about her different sexual experiences, which includes questions and answers like these: "Have you ever kissed someone of the same sex? Yes. Have you ever done something you regretted? Yes. Are you a virgin? No comment." And she's only 16.

And everything is in plain view for the whole world to see.

Welcome to the new virtual world called MySpace. Much like Ralph's Diner on *Happy Days*, MySpace is the new hangout for characters like Potsie, Richie, Fonzi, and their closest 100 million friends. It's an online community that is part chat room, part movie theater, part shopping mall, part bar, part concert, and part slumber party. But unlike the neighborhood skating rink or bowling alley, it is open 24 hours a day, 7 days a week, 365 days a year. Because each profile is a blank canvas for its owner, it is a place for everyone to express his or her individuality. It is called MySpace because it is literally "your space"—you can do with it whatever you please.

Even though MySpace is hesitant to release the exact age breakdown of its users, probably about 80 percent of the profiles are of adults 18 and older. The remaining 20 percent are teenagers between the age of 14 and 17.[1] While that doesn't sound like a very big following, you have to remember that MySpace has more than 100 million users—more than the combined population of California, Texas, and New York—and is growing at about three million new profiles a month. That means that approximately 20 million teenagers are going through this social network to talk about their breakups, to blog about schoolwork and music, and to find the address of the closest party.

The amazing thing about the MySpace social phenomenon is the speed at which it has gathered such a loyal following. In less than three years, MySpace has become the second-most visited site on the Internet (behind Yahoo), has been sold for more than $580 million to Rupert Murdoch's News Corporation, and has become the new place for meeting people and exchanging information. What's even more amazing is that most parents are ignorant, skeptical, or oblivious that MySpace even exists.

Family Values

Our culture doesn't often recognize the family as the fundamental building block of society. But without it, our basic values and faith break down. God designed the family unit to help nurture and cultivate the next generation of leaders, to provide guidance and discernment, and to instill love and spiritual truths in our children. It wasn't by accident that God used the imagery of family to explain our relationship to Him. He is our Father, and we are His sons and daughters.

Proverbs 22:6 (NASB) eloquently notes, "Train up a child in the way he should go, even when he is old he will not depart from it." As you probably already know, this wise advice is much easier to discuss than to implement. Today's kids face challenges that were nonexistent when we were youngsters. The Internet, cable television, and lifelike video games make parenting more difficult than ever before. Relating to teenagers today is like climbing a greased pole—slippery, challenging, and often discouraging. But it is absolutely necessary if you are going to influence their lives. Josh Billings once said, "To bring up a child in the way he should go, travel that way yourself once in a while."[2] In this spirit we are going to immerse ourselves in the MySpace community so that we can better understand our kids and our responsibilities.

Although I don't have kids of my own yet (*yet* being the key word), I feel like a parent because I've been speaking all over the country for the last decade on issues that affect kids. I'm like a surrogate parent or an older brother to many of them. Whether I'm talking about sex, peer pressure, or MySpace, I've learned that many teenagers don't connect with their parents or don't believe their parents even care. I was recently approached by a frustrated middle-school girl who said she was struggling with depression and suicide. When I asked if she had discussed these issues with her parents, she said her mom told her to "stop whining and suck it up." In another situation, I received an e-mail through my MySpace account from a 14-year-old girl who was asking questions about premarital sex. She stated in her e-mail that "I would love to talk to my mom about this, but she just seems so perfect. She doesn't get me."

Please understand that I'm not going to tell you how to raise your children. I'm simply here to share my experiences with the MySpace community, answer questions that I've received from parents and teens alike, and help you protect and connect with your kids. My number one priority is the safety of your family. Think of me as a translator and a guide. You are about to dive into unchartered virtual waters—I'm here to help you freshen up on your strokes.

People naturally fear what they do not understand. Because of the negative press this online community has received recently, parents assume that MySpace is inherently bad. Not the case. Like any other piece of technology—the Internet, e-mail, cell phones— MySpace is simply a tool for leveraging communication and sharing information. But unfortunately, the better the tool is at effective communication, the worse it is when used improperly. This is certainly the case with MySpace. Used correctly, it can be a wonderful resource to talk to teenagers, share in their struggles, encourage their dreams, and nurture their growth. But used poorly, it can be equally destructive to teenagers' overall development. We're here to make sure the latter doesn't happen.

After speaking to thousands of people about MySpace, I've learned that most parents fall into one of three categories. They are (1) ignorant that MySpace even exists, thus having little or no influence in their teenager's virtual life; (2) angry that it is a teen hangout, often verbally sparring with their kids to stop them from using it; or (3) cautious of the new technology but trying to understand and willing to participate in the new world. The majority of parents fall into the first two categories, but the successful ones fall into the third. Regardless of how you feel about the Internet and online communities, they are here to stay. Even if MySpace was shut down tomorrow, more than a dozen other ones, including

Facebook, Xanga, Friendster, and MyYearbook, are waiting to take its place. You don't have to blindly accept everything that transpires online, but you'll be a better parent if you understand it.

We don't stop our children from driving even though automobile accidents account for more teenage deaths than any other cause, with 3657 American teens between the ages of 15 and 20 dying in 2003.[3] Likewise, we're not going to stop our teenagers from chatting online and meeting new people. We just need to teach them how to do it properly so that they don't get hurt.

Perspective, Priorities, and the Plan

John Wilmot, the Earl of Rochester, once joked, "Before I got married I had six theories about bringing up children; now I have six children, and no theories." Whether you have teenagers, are about to have teenagers, or just yell at the neighborhood teens from your front porch, you probably realize you are dealing with a rowdy bunch. You may feel as if you're herding cats, and most teens I deal with have the attention span of a sea monkey. So if you are truly interested in influencing them, you'll need a detailed plan of action.

I know no better place to search for this plan than the Bible. Even though it doesn't speak specifically about online issues—where was Moses on that one!—it speaks at great lengths about raising children and loving relationships. Most parents are struggling to grasp MySpace, but a handful of parents are doing it well already. By leveraging their expertise and using the Word as a blueprint, I have been able to construct a solid outline that will help you on your journey. If you study it closely, you will see that this outline will not only help you navigate the good, bad, and ugly of MySpace, but it will also help you confront many other issues that may arise with your teenager.

The plan of action has three parts:

Perspective. As we mentioned at the beginning of the chapter, children are a gift from the Lord. They are on loan from God, meaning that they are really His children that we have the opportunity to raise and nurture. This is important to address from the outset so we remember that our responsibility is limited. We are called to follow Scripture, listen to God's leading in our lives, and do everything in our power to protect, comfort, and lead our kids, but ultimately, only God can make them grow. I often speak to parents who are heartbroken that their kids have made mistakes, but they fail to realize they are not called to control their children's lives. They are called to guide them.

The second part of gaining perspective deals with walking in their shoes. You will relate more effectively to your children if you are actively involved in all aspects of their lives. Parents can't expect their teenagers to heed their advice if the parents are not willing to try to understand their kids' situation. If you want to offer powerful guidance about MySpace and online communications, try to understand as much of it as possible. You cannot impart wisdom you do not possess. Your teen will respect your insight much more if you know how to navigate the site, appreciate its benefits, and understand its problems. As leadership guru Stephen Covey noted in his bestselling book *The Seven Habits of Highly Effective People,* "Seek first to understand...then to be understood."[4] In the first few chapters of this book, we are going examine the dynamic landscape around MySpace so that we can have a clear perspective before learning the basics.

Priorities. The fundamental, biblical principles for raising a child aren't circumstantial. They are eternal. They don't change with new technologies, new theories, or new families. Scripture clearly calls us to love, discipline, teach, guide, protect, nurture, and develop our children. Providing for their physical needs can be a real challenge, but we all know that providing for their spiritual and moral development is even more difficult.

Every teenager is unique, and their needs and desires change often and drastically. As a parent, you are responsible to make sure your child's continued development aligns with the growth of your whole family. Because situations are different, you will have to decide what you will allow your children to do online and how they will do it. Most parents wisely restrict their teenagers from roaming freely on the Internet. But the nature and extent of those controls will differ from family to family.

In the second section of the book, we are going to take a guided tour through MySpace so you can make an informed decision. I'll teach you how to log onto different accounts, how to follow your child's electronic footprints, and even how to set up your own account. By the end of the section, you should be comfortable reading blogs, surfing chat rooms, posting comments, and listening to music.

Plan. All of our education and discussion would be worthless if we didn't formulate a plan for implementing our newfound knowledge. Privacy and protection are most parents' key concerns. But if we just stop there, we may be neglecting the greatest power of MySpace. Believe it or not, MySpace can be a great tool for parents. It can be a second pair of eyes and ears for those who want to better understand their children and the challenges they face. Parents can use this virtual community to monitor, interact with, and encourage their kids like never before.

In many instances, MySpace doesn't create problems, it simply reveals them. Teenagers face difficult decisions and peer pressure nearly every day. Some parents don't want to admit that their children struggle with sexual temptations, drinking opportunities, drug-related issues, depression, or loneliness. But most teenagers do face most of these pressures. In the past, parents were able to turn a blind eye to these issues and act as if they didn't exist. But in the virtual world, teens are writing down their problems and reaching out for help. Instead of guessing about or ignoring the issues that teenagers have, we have the unique opportunity through portals such as MySpace to understand their problems and provide help.

In the last part of the book, I hope to help you formulate a plan to work with your kids. I can't possibly prepare you for all the struggles you may face, but by providing a map and showing you how to use it, I can point you in the right direction. Ironically, most teenagers don't need you to *do* anything. They just need you to *be* there for them. We'll discuss different online situations, relay a few success stories from other parents, suggest options regarding talking to your teen, and provide resources for your continual walk.

《《 》》

If I have learned anything in all my years dealing with teenagers, it is this: They are smart. *Really* smart. Smarter than we give them credit for. Because of the information age and access to different forms of media, they display a great capacity to learn, and they are not afraid to dig for the answers they seek. The struggles we faced when we were 18, they are facing when they are 12. Whether we like it or not, their intellectual maturation is light-years beyond where we were at that same age. The problem is that many teens do not have a firm spiritual and moral foundation to help them make wise decisions. They can tell you ten different positions in which to have sex, but they can't tell you why God designed it for marriage. They can tell you that Jesus died on the cross, but they can't tell you why He did so. They can tell you that talking on the cell phone, IMing their buddies, e-mailing their girlfriends, surfing on the Web, and hanging out on MySpace is cool, but they can't tell you why they like it or explain the dangers behind it.

Our job is to determine the why. When we figure out why, we can formulate a plan to monitor how they participate in this whole new world called MySpace.

Let's get started…

Friends and Fiends

The Thin Line Between Schoolmates and Strangers

Fathers, do not exasperate your children; instead, bring them up in the training and instruction of the Lord.

EPHESIANS 6:4

ONE OF GOD'S AMAZING QUALITIES is that He just tells it like it is. Regardless of whether the news is good or bad, positive or negative, inspirational or depressing, He just tells it like it is. When God told Abraham, "Know for certain that your descendents will be strangers in a country not their own, and they will be enslaved and mistreated four hundred years" (Genesis 15:13), He did not preface it by saying, "Now, don't take this personally," or "It's not really going to be that bad." He just told Abraham the truth. Likewise, when Jesus said, "I am the way and the truth and the life. No one comes to the Father except through me" (John 14:6), He didn't say "Unless, of course, you struggle with just having one God—then take any road you like," or "Make sure you examine all the other options first." In His goodness, God tells us the truth so we are fully aware of the blessings and dangers we may face. He is the great I AM, and His Word is the great IT IS.

If we want to really know our children and be involved in their lives, we have to face the truth, especially as it pertains to things like MySpace. If we don't have a clear understanding of this communication tool, we won't know the truth, and we won't be able to pass the truth on to our children. As I mentioned before, MySpace isn't necessarily good or bad, but how a teenager uses MySpace can be good or bad. If we can educate ourselves on both the dangers and the opportunities, we will be well-equipped to be the spiritual guides and parents God has called us to be.

MySpace can be compared to a large American city. It has lots of good places and a few bad places, lots of good people but a few very bad people as well. We need to teach our kids how to tell the difference.

The Media and MySpace

If your only education about MySpace has come through the media, you probably have a pretty lopsided view of this vibrant online community. Because of its booming growth and recent problems, news desks and radio stations have targeted MySpace as a place that harbors sexual predators, allows profanity, shows sexual content, and exercises little or no caution. Concerns usually fall into two categories—content and connections. People are concerned about the type of content a teen can view, and they are concerned about the type of connections a teen can make. But before we jump to conclusions, let's examine a few of the disheartening reports to gain some valuable perspective.

Let there be no mistake. Unfortunate cases of teen exploitation do exist, and these are a concern. In February 2006, Connecticut Attorney General Richard Blumenthal said MySpace was "a parent's worst nightmare" and announced a criminal probe into the service's activities. His office had received reports that as many as seven underage girls in the state had questionable sexual contact with adult men they met on the site. From their reports, all the girls lied about their age.[1]

Also in 2006, Nathan Contos, a 26-year-old man in Santa Cruz, California, was arrested for molesting a 14-year-old girl he met on MySpace while allegedly posing as a teenager himself.[2] Ray Eidem is charged with attempted rape of a child in Vancouver, Washington, in a MySpace-related case.[3] And *Wired News* ran the names of some registered sex offenders in San Francisco and neighboring Sonoma County. Five of the men had MySpace pages, and their names, photographs, ages, astrological signs, and locations matched their profiles on the state's online sex offender registry.[4]

If the backlash against MySpace was just focused on the tragic problem of sexual predators and online perpetrators, at least the problem would be confined. Unfortunately, numerous reports indicate that MySpace is also a breeding ground for violence, insubordination, and hate. In April 2006, on the seventh anniversary of the Columbine school shootings, five Kansas students were arrested for plotting a similar massacre and discussing it on MySpace.[5] The American Civil Liberties Union (ACLU) is handling a case in Pennsylvania where Hazel Scantling was suspended from school for posting vulgar comments about her teachers and classmates.[6] East Grand Rapids High School in Michigan temporarily prohibited about 20 students from participating in extracurricular activities after seeing an online photo of them drinking.[7] Even NBC's *Dateline* pressed the panic button by calling MySpace "a cyber secret teenagers keep from tech-challenged parents."[8]

With all of this disturbing information circling, we need to ask ourselves some important questions: Are these isolated incidents, or are they a reflection of the whole online community? Are a hundred serious cases representative of the other 99,999,900 accounts? Should we ban our teenagers from participating in an environment that may have some questionable material? Are teens wise enough to make good decisions while being loosely supervised?

The flood of recent reports may feel like an epidemic, but when put in context, it is probably overblown. The number of incidents linked to MySpace is considerably lower than the number of real-world cases. According to a National Center of Juvenile Justice report based on an analysis of data collected by the FBI, about 15,700 statutory rapes were reported to the authorities in the United States in 2000. That is about 43 cases per day. California, a state with a population of 33 million, averaged 62 rape convictions a month in the late 1990s.[9] MySpace currently has 100 million members and has far fewer reported rape allegations. We might argue that being on MySpace is safer than living in California!

To put things in perspective, go to www.familywatchdog.us and type in your home address. Familywatchdog.us is a national registry of sex offenders and predators, and the site will display a map of all the known offenders within a ten-mile radius of your home. What you will see will shock you. All the people I know who have entered in their home address have pulled up several sex offenders in their areas. One of my friends has a three-year-old boy. When the dad typed in his home address, which is in a very safe North Dallas neighborhood, he found 56 registered sex offenders within ten miles of his home. That means that 56 pairs of convicted eyes could be watching his boy play in the yard, swim in the pool, and walk with his mother. The reason that many parents have been so distraught about MySpace is that the media have brought it to their attention and caused a panic. Most parents don't realize that their kids are surrounded by bigger potential problems every day. What is more troubling—ten sex offenders 10 miles away or ten sex offenders 10,000 miles away? It is something to think about.

Unfortunately, of all the news reports I have read, none have highlighted the positive ministries and connections that are taking place on MySpace. I've never heard CNN talk about Acts 242, a community of trust and servanthood dedicated to facilitating relationships with Christ, or the D.O.G. (Disciples of God) Pound Ministry, a teen-oriented site that leaves encouraging Scripture on kid's personal pages. I've never heard ABC mention that most Christian music artists have their official fan sites on MySpace, including Jeremy Camp, who has over 42,000 friends on his page. I've never heard *USA Today* mention how many people use their sites to support groups like the Boys and Girls Clubs, Big Brothers Big Sisters of America, the Special Olympics, the Susan G. Komen Breast Cancer Foundation, or children's hospitals. And these are just a few examples that I've experienced with my close-knit group of friends. I'm sure many other ministries and organizations benefit from the MySpace community.

Though the media have been quick to invoke fear into parents' hearts, they have been slow to remind them that more than one-third of MySpace's staff is dedicated to protection and privacy, and that the company has recently hired Hemanshu Nigam, the former director of consumer security outreach and safe computing at Microsoft, as their chief security officer. In addition to working for unquestionably the most powerful software company in the world—Microsoft—Nigam was a federal prosecutor and was an adviser to the White House on cyber stalking. MySpace is also testing software that will scan each picture loaded onto their site to make sure too much skin isn't showing. Not bad for a company who reportedly doesn't care.

Please understand that I'm not advocating that we let teens run willy-nilly all over the Internet. The amount of personal information that is floating around MySpace, including full names, street addresses, and phone numbers, is not safe. We need to protect today's youth. We *have* to protect them—we are instructed by God to protect them. But protect them from what? From the system, from predators, or from themselves? This is what we have to figure out.

No Need to Panic

Mary Gray, an assistant professor at Indiana University who researches new media, said the current "hysteria" over MySpace is nothing new.[10] It is similar to the comic book outrage in the 1950s, when parents found out that some of the drawings were violent and bloody; the Beatles hysteria in the 1960s, when rock 'n' roll started taking the place of good, wholesome gospel music; the MTV era of the 1980s, when our kids wanted to grow out their hair and bang their heads like rockers; or the Internet boom of the 1990s, when teenagers could roam freely all over the world, searching for everything from proms to pyramids. Every time a new medium is introduced, it garners attention. And when problems arise, we are quick to place blame on the new technology, when in reality, the same problems we have always had are simply revealing themselves in new ways.

But if you are a parent and you truly love your children, you shouldn't be satisfied hearing that MySpace is only a phase or a fad and that it too will pass. You should want specifics on the current situation so that your kids don't just survive but thrive. Teens will most likely survive the MySpace craze regardless of what happens, but as with previous cultural shifts, some kids adapt better than others. As Christians, we are called to a higher standard, which we want to impart to our children: "Be perfect, therefore, as your heavenly Father is perfect" (Matthew 5:48).

Many parents have stopped me, called me, and e-mailed me with questions regarding MySpace and their teenagers. Everybody has an opinion on MySpace, but unfortunately, many people have gone to the extreme with their views, either demanding that it be shut down or hailing it as flawless. Neither extreme is healthy. In an effort to uncover the truth about MySpace, MSNBC's *The Red Tape Chronicles* investigated the site and invited Bob Sullivan, the author of *Your Evil Twin: Behind the Identity Theft Epidemic,* to offer some commentary on it.[11] Readers then had a chance to write in with their thoughts. I've included a few of the readers' opinions below:

Opinions on MySpace

> I'm sorry, but I don't think someone who goes on MySpace and is not smart enough to no that u don't give out ur number or address to anyone should go on the site. I am sick of people blaming other people for not keeping an eye on what ur kids do on the computer, in ur house, under ur own nose. I also believe that the lawsuits people are filing against MySpace are getting out of control. Please stop people from looking for that easy buck.
>
> ANONYMOUS

> MySpace is treading on dangerous ground and if they don't take these issues seriously they will find themselves

out of business in the very near future. They may be thinking "with 85 million customers...that will never happen!" Well, it's quite amazing what one case and a few court rulings can do. I have disliked the site from its start and would welcome (along w/ most parents in this country) the end of MySpace. While the concept is great, safety is impossible to control in a world plagued by sexual predators and other criminals. I have no doubt that MySpace has single-handedly contributed to thousands of sexual assaults and other violence all over the world. Unfortunately, only a few incidents a month make the news. It really is time for MySpace to end.

BOB, LOS ANGELES, CA

I think it is ridiculous how everyone rags on MySpace. Shouldn't it be the responsibility of...oh, I don't know... these 14-year-old girls' PARENTS to monitor what they are doing? Why should the website be responsible? Parents need to pay more attention. MySpace is not the problem...poor parenting is! I see outrageous pictures of 15-yro's in their bikinis. Not only are these girls ASKING for trouble...they are obviously not being monitored. Blame the parents and their poor parenting.

RAINA, MIDDLETOWN, NY

People need to take responsibility for their own actions...whether it is their own bad judgment or their bad parenting. The last thing we need is the government regulating everything we do or see. STOP BLAMING EVERYONE ELSE!

ANONYMOUS

Yes, in my opinion, the ultimate responsibility for what children do online rests with the parents; but, the fact is, parents are neither omnipotent nor always present. Frankly, in my opinion, many parents aren't that good at parenting anyway and are not very aware. (In fact, many parents are counseled to NOT be too involved in what their kids do for fear of being too controlling!) There's also a delicate balance that must be observed as a parent: How to guide your child to the right choices without pushing him/her away. It's not MySpace's province to give instruction in parenting, but it is MySpace's responsibility to not profit from the error-prone, immature, or predatory nature of many of its members.

TJM, PORTLAND, OR

What about parental responsibility? Parents should monitor their children's Internet usage and enforce their own personal MySpace policies, whether their children are not allowed to use it or are allowed to use it with restrictions.

With all the children posting inappropriate pictures and reporting drug and alcohol use (should we ban alcohol because, like MySpace, some children lie about their age and use it?), it is obvious that these parents are doing a poor job of supervising their children in multiple areas. With MySpace, however, these parents have someone else to blame, which may be comforting to them and give them a false feeling of security.

JENNIFER, DURHAM, NC

Like many of society's ills, this is the result of a parenting failure. My generation's parents used the TV as a babysitter, and now my generation is using the computer as its babysitter. But the computer is a bigger threat to your child's well-being.

What to do? Put the computer in the living room, keep an eye on what your children are doing on the Internet, and learn to read the computer's history to see where your children have been. Limit their time online, and insist that you meet any friend they correspond with via e-mail or IM. You can try telling your kids about "stranger danger" all you want, but kids are convinced they know better, and nothing bad will happen to them. Thus it is a parent's duty to protect children as much as possible.

I can't protect my kids from the common cold, skinned knees, or the heartaches of life, but I'll do what it takes to keep them away from predators.

MNEMENTH, CALLAHAN, FL

I actually have 3 kids and monitor everything they do. I also teach my kids to be open and honest with me. I agree with what you are saying. People need to stop suing for stupid stuff, like the fact that you are getting fat b/c you eat fried chicken and that your child runs away b/c you are out of touch with them. Wake up, America, and take responsibility for your own actions.

KATE, JACKSONVILLE, AL

We need to explore just how much the parents are responsible for what their children are doing on the Internet. You can blame MySpace all you want, but the reality is—if children aren't being looked after properly in the home, they are going to find a way to get into trouble, online or off. Long before MySpace was ever around, there was instant messaging and chat rooms, and the same stuff has been going on in those for years. Like anything else, MySpace is what you allow it to be. My 15-year-old niece has a page on it, and I signed up for one as well (I am 35). Her mother also has one. And we keep tabs on her every move. I think if you're going to let your kids have access to a site like MySpace, it's your responsibility to monitor what goes on there. It's called being a grown-up. If children are getting on planes and flying across the country to meet strange men, maybe Mom and Dad need to get involved in the child's life a little more and stop letting the computer and the television raise their kid. It's amazing how much we are blaming technology for how our children are turning out these days...they're overweight, they are oversexed at too young of age, their priorities are all out of whack, they are sitting in front of the computer or television with their iPod stuck in their ears for hours on end...it's de-socializing them, etc, etc. Where are the parents that are allowing them to access these things?

The bottom line is, stop blaming technology and stop trying to be your kid's "buddy" and be an active, clued in parent! When I was a child, my parents knew where I was, who I was with, and what I was doing at all times. It was their job to know. Maybe the question we should be asking is, where are the parents and why don't they know what's going on with their kids?

CAROLINE, NASHVILLE, TN

WOW! I think the first comment says a lot about the kind of people who use MySpace.com: illiterate, unintelligent, and unable to take responsibility. MySpace has made its reputation, and now that reputation is going to lead to its demise. My 14-year-old son said he wouldn't use the site because it is full of "scumbags." Enough said.

ANONYMOUS

Okay. Here's the solution. Charge money. It's as simple as that. Kids under 16 won't be able to afford the fee, and teenagers without a job won't be able to go online. No more child predators because there won't be any since there are no more kids online anymore. Sure, MySpace would crash, but I would give up anything to not hear another 14-year-old girl being sexually assaulted or raped. Here are some more suggestions: The use of a Social Security number that would restrict anyone under 16. No more lying, but with all the ID thefts, that might not work for long. Then there's the use of credit cards. The porno industry uses this and keeps kids off limits. Why shouldn't MySpace? There's a solution to everything, even if it means killing the site. MySpace should quit putting kids in danger in order to make money. That's just low and shady business. For the people that are suing, making money off your child's pain is not the way to go, but fighting to force the site out of business is. There's power in numbers, I suggest you use them.

JULIO, DANVILLE, KY

As you can see, people from all over the country are divided about the steps we should take to protect our children. But the common thread is that we *should* protect our children and that parents bear a significant portion of the responsibility for their kids' actions. MySpace is not inherently evil—it is simply a tool that can be used for fellowship and communication. The type of communication, whether good or bad, is determined by the user.

Is a gun bad because it kills? Not necessarily. In fact, it is quite a useful weapon if you are about to be mauled by a bear. But if it is used incorrectly, it can empower someone to murder his neighbor.

The same can be said about MySpace. It is a wonderful communication tool for teens to keep up with one another, express their creativity, and explore the online world. But if kids are left unsupervised, MySpace can lead to their demise.

《‹‹ ››》

One of the main problems with MySpace is not the technology but the users. Users can lie, manipulate, and deceive one another. Most people don't do those things to intentionally hurt other people. They lie about their age, income, or profession to protect their pride. Many people are uncomfortable in their own skin, so they exaggerate their profiles to make themselves sound more intelligent, more beautiful, or more desirable than they really are.

Teens often exaggerate for the same reasons. They desperately want to be liked and want to be part of the in crowd. Kids go through many phases in the growth process and often experiment with their personalities and characteristics in an effort to find themselves. For the most part, this is a natural and healthy process, but danger creeps in when the people molding and influencing kids are not the parents but online strangers. We want our kids to find themselves, but we don't want them to be found by others, either physically or emotionally. We can't control what other people are going to do or how they are going to use MySpace, but we can guide our kids to make sure they are not easy targets.

3

My House Is Not a Democracy

Virtual Parents and Virtual Tyrants

Do not withhold discipline from a child;
if you punish him with a rod, he will not die.

PROVERBS 23:13

IF YOU HAD A 14-YEAR-OLD DAUGHTER, would you let her talk on the Internet, virtually unmonitored, to someone she doesn't know? I can understand that she might be able to hide her "virtual stud" from you for a couple days or weeks, but don't you think you would grow a little suspicious if she was glued to the computer screen for a couple months? And when she asked if it was okay for someone to pick her up from school, take her to dinner and a movie, and bring her home, would you not even ask to meet the guy or find out how they connected? Would you not care about where they were going to dinner or what time she was going to be home? Would you not even be curious about the age of the boy who would be picking up your precious little girl?

I only ask because this is exactly the scenario that transpired with a 14-year-old girl from Austin, Texas. She met a 19-year-old guy on MySpace who was posing as a high school senior, talked to him for a couple months online, met him after school, went to dinner and movie, and was later sexually assaulted. And her mom is claiming that she knew nothing about the whole incident. Now, the girl and her mother are suing MySpace for $30 million, claiming that the company was responsible to protect the teen.[1]

Or try this scenario on for size—if your 16-year-old daughter came to you and said she needed a passport, would you just trot down to the post office and help her get one? If she said that she needed it for a school trip to Canada—because lots of classes take trips to Canada, right?—would you just blindly assume that she was telling the truth? Wouldn't you at least ask to see the permission slip or call another parent and say, "Hey, what's the deal about the school trip to the frozen tundra?" Wouldn't you think it was a little odd that your girl was asking for a document that would allow her to travel internationally?

The parents of a 16-year-old honors student from Michigan chose not to ask these basic questions, so you can imagine the field day that the media had when their little girl hopped a plane to the Middle East to meet a guy she had been chatting with on MySpace.[2] And somehow, MySpace got blamed for all of this.

After reading these two ridiculous events, which the parents could easily have prevented had they at least had a clue, you have to ask, are these MySpace problems, or are they parental issues?

My thoughts and prayers go out to the teen who was molested—*nobody* ever deserves to be sexually assaulted—but my question is, where were the parents in all of this? MySpace certainly needs to take every possible precaution to protect its users, but they are not virtual babysitters or parents, responsible for following kids around both the Internet and the real world. Where was this girl's mother during all of this? Shouldn't she know where her daughter is and ask questions about her well-being? It wasn't as if the 19-year-old guy broke into their house, held the family at gunpoint, and raped the daughter. He picked her up right in front of the mother's nose!

And I can understand if you lose track of your 16-year-old at the mall for a couple minutes. Teens have a habit of wandering off. But to lose her to the Middle East and have United States officials reroute her back from Amman, Jordan? A well-trained pigeon can be taught to watch your children better than that! There is simply no excuse for this type of lackluster parenting.

But these are the examples that the media are highlighting to explain the dangers of MySpace. Of course, after reading the details, MySpace doesn't appear to be solely responsible in either one of these situations. Each tragic event provided multiple opportunities for a parent to step in and bring the madness to a halt. But no one did. And children were hurt as a result.

I want to make this point as clear as possible so that nobody misses it—*you,* the parents, are ultimately responsible for your children's growth and well-being. God has entrusted them to you and empowered you to be their guardian, protector, provider, and leader. No Scripture allows you to default on your responsibility or shift it to another source, such as culture, the television, or the Internet. When you stand before the Lord, He will hold you accountable for your godly influence on your children—or your lack therof.

In the Old Testament, Eli was considered a successful priest, but his parenting left much to be desired. When he did not correct his sons for their outlandish behavior, God said, "For I told him that I would judge his family forever because of the sin he knew about; his sons made themselves contemptible, and he failed to restrain them" (1 Samuel 3:13). Because Eli did not take his parental duties seriously, both his children and his family suffered. The same will happen with our families if we do not step up to the plate.

Dr. Tony Evans, the senior pastor at Oak Cliff Bible Fellowship in Dallas, Texas, often states, "My house is not a democracy. My kids don't get to vote on how I'm going to raise or punish them. And when they do vote, it doesn't count!" Although the congregation often laughs, Dr. Evans is speaking the truth. He understands his immense responsibility and knows he is called to be a father, not just a friend to his children.

Our American culture has given kids too much power and granted them too many rights. I didn't get to vote on my bedtime. I didn't get to vote on whether or not to eat my green beans. I didn't get to vote on going to school. My parents made me do these things. And for good reason. They wanted me to become a godly man, capable of making wise and discerning choices, and they knew that the right road was not always the easy one. More than anything, they knew their role as parents was to imitate God's role as the Father—to be protectors, providers, and when necessary, enforcers of holy behavior.

One mother hit the nail on the head when she said to me, "MySpace executives can't be responsible for raising every child in America." I couldn't agree with her more. Throughout the rest of the book, we are going to talk about what MySpace is doing and should be doing to protect your teens. But all of that is secondary to your role as parents, especially as Christian parents. If you don't build an internal parenting system to guide your son or daughter, MySpace can do nothing to pick up the slack. MySpace's responsibility should complement your parenting, not replace it. You can't rely on somebody else to raise your kid—that is your job.

Most people who are taking the time to read this book are probably already good parents, so I don't want to spend too much time on parental responsibilities. I just want to remind you of three scriptural keys that you possess that will help you unlock the virtual world.

Patience

The first characteristic of love that Paul wanted us to remember is this: "Love is patient" (1 Corinthians 13:4). This is not by accident. Paul understood that patience will cover a multitude of sins and struggles as we simply wait in quiet discernment for a clearer understanding.

In our overly sensationalized culture, everything is urgent, and situations often get overblown. The media have pushed the MySpace panic button, and people are jumping on the bandwagon to dump on the website. Many parents don't even know what they are scared about; they just know that *Dateline* and CNN have said some pretty disturbing things about this MySpace thingy. Parents certainly need to take some extra precautions to protect their kids, but some parents don't even know who or what they are protecting their kids from. This is not thoughtful discernment; it's erratic hysteria.

The situation escalates when parents check out their kids' MySpace account and see unruly pictures, off-color comments, and personal information. Instead of taking a step back and trying to understand the situation, some parents quickly reprimand their children for being foolish or dumb. They pour gas on an already flammable situation.

Don't get me wrong—parents *do* need to handle some situations swiftly and aggressively. If your daughter is chatting with an unknown adult online or your son has pornographic pictures on his account, you need to bring the behavior to a screeching halt and *then* figure out the root of the problem. Situations that threaten your kids' physical or emotional safety demand quick action. But for many Christian parents, the situation will not be this dire. Many kids who are surfing the pages of MySpace are not troublemakers. They are just curious, creative, and hormone-laden teens who are trying to find themselves. They don't need a tongue lashing; they need a gentle reminder of their godly character and responsibility.

Paul chose patience as his first characteristic of love because he understood that people's actions are external symptoms of their internal conditions. The things you will see and experience on your child's MySpace profile are visible manifestations of what's going on in his or her heart and spirit. If you deal solely with the problem at hand—the fact that she has too much personal information, his language is too crass, her pictures are too revealing—you may miss the root of the problem, which is probably some type of emptiness inside. As parents, we need to address the real problem and not just the symptoms.

You will sometimes need to act quickly to protect your teen, and at other times you will need to exercise a little more patience. The key is being able to tell the difference. If you are not sure, always err on the side of being a little more aggressive. You will never regret being slightly more overprotective than you need to be.

But remember, these kids are teenagers and are just trying to have a little fun. Your parents didn't always "get" you either, especially when you wanted to listen to that "rock 'n' roll devil music." Your house is not a democracy, but give kids some freedom to roam underneath your watchful eye.

Honesty

If you want your teens to act with integrity and speak honestly, you have to model that behavior to them.

A mother in Santa Rosa, California, set up a fictitious account as a 16-year-old girl on MySpace—with the screen name "Candy Sweetness"—to test her two teenage sons. Her goal was to see if they would reveal any personal or private information. After numerous e-mails back and forth, one of her boys gave up his phone number. She exposed her teens on an episode of *Dr. Phil* that examined online sexual predators.

If you are thinking *Good for her!* you are the parents I'm talking to right now. This is *not* the type of behavior that builds trust and rapport with your kids. We are not spying on our kids! We are parenting. We are monitoring with the intent of teaching, correcting, and rebuking. We are staying actively involved in their lives in hopes of modeling Christlike behavior in all aspects of living.

The difference between spying and monitoring is intent. If you are spying on your kids, your intent is to deceive them by either not letting them know you are around or by acting like you are someone you're not. This is not appropriate behavior for adults. I'm sure that this mother's two boys not only were horrified to find out that their mother lied to them by posing as "Candy Sweetness" but also were twice as embarrassed to have her secret revealed to them on national television. What kind of message do you think that sends to your children? "I don't trust you, and I'm going to embarrass you when you do wrong"? How does that help?

MySpace does have some shady users, and some dangerous information is floating around in the community, but these dangers are magnified tenfold on the rest of the Internet. And you can't track your kids all over the World Wide Web. If you try to act sly and coy, don't be surprised if your kids disappear from MySpace and get involved in a much more dangerous underground virtual community. You will have pushed them there with your characterless behavior.

Your house is not a democracy, but you still need to lovingly encourage your children and give them room to grow. If you rule with an iron fist, your teenage girl will more likely revolt in every way possible by wearing black eye makeup, dating the most rebellious drug dealer at school, and listening to Marilyn Manson. Good parents give their children a healthy amount of room to experiment and be creative in the real world. This same rule should apply to the virtual world.

Larry Estes, a computer software developer from Houston, Texas, and his wife, Lisa, have a very different approach to monitoring their three kids, ages 11, 13, and 16. Instead of spying on them, they have been very open at establishing a "zero expectation of privacy" policy around their house. In addition to placing monitoring technology on their computers, they have told their kids that they should be prepared for one of them to look over their shoulder or ask a question about their online activity at any time. "We feel education is the best form of control," Larry says. "If we tried to control everything, they would just go out and seek it somewhere else."[3]

I happen to agree with the Estes family, and if I were a gambling man, I'd bet that their children avoid most online problems because of their approach. Be honest with your kids about why you are monitoring their behavior, and they will be more likely to be transparent about their activities.

Discipline

When I was growing up, I learned very quickly not to confuse my parent's kindness with weakness. As long as I was playing by their rules, everything was great, but as soon as I tried to do something stupid or inconsiderate, the game was over. When I was about 16 years old, I thought I was tough enough to call my mother a derogatory term. Little did I know that my dad doubled as a steeplechase trainer in his past life, and after leaping over the kitchen table, he pinned me against the wall. With my toes dangling six inches off the ground, I realized I had overstepped my bounds.

My parents were never harsh when they disciplined their three boys, but they were always firm. Although I didn't realize it at the time, they allowed us to have a little bit of freedom so that we would learn how to navigate the rough waters of life on our own. Most of the time we did pretty well. Sometimes we struggled. And on occasion, we stumbled off the path. But all of our experiences helped mold us into the godly men we are today. Momma Illian always said, "It's all part of parenting. You try to help your children avoid the big mistakes and hope they learn from the small ones."

Teenagers are like the dinosaur raptors from the movie *Jurrasic Park*. Although high-voltage electric fences surrounded the raptors, they strategically tested each fence to find weaknesses in the system. Your teens will do the same thing. They will test the boundaries to see if your system has any weaknesses, to see if you will stand firm on your beliefs. If you, or you and your spouse, don't set rules and stick by them, your teenager will break free and wreak havoc on the family.

Ephesians 6:4 (NASB) states, "Fathers, do not provoke your children to anger; but bring them up in the discipline and instruction of the Lord." As most parents already know, disciplining your teens is easy if you don't mind making them angry. But that is not what the Lord wants. He asks us to discipline and instruct our kids without provoking them to anger. This is a much more difficult task. It requires faith, careful insight, understanding, and compassion.

If you want to set realistic MySpace guidelines for your kids without exasperating them, you are going to have to take some time to understand the online community. Some kids have the maturity to be loosely monitored; others need to be hounded like a bird dog. Whether your teens fall into the first or second category will depend on how you measure their emotional and spiritual intelligence as well as where you feel God leading your family. You may decide that

MySpace is okay for your children or you may not. But either way, you need to have concrete, biblical reasons for why you believe what you do, and you need to be able to communicate them to your teen. Answers like "Because I said so" or "MySpace is evil" are not going to cut it. Kids don't respect that, nor should they. If we are truly being guided by the Holy Spirit in all of our decisions, we should be able to explain at least a small portion of our decision.

Does this mean you have to explain all your disciplinary rules to your children? Of course not. They don't need to know all the small details regarding your decisions, but they do need to know that you thoughtfully and prayerfully examined each situation without simply jumping to conclusions. If they see your pattern of constantly examining each situation and taking it to the Lord before making a decision, they will be likely to implement that decision-making process in their lives as well. And that is what parenting is all about.

When you effectively monitor your children and cultivate their growth, you don't have to come down on them like a hammer every time they step out of line. Just because other teenagers are acting stupid on MySpace doesn't mean your child is doing the same. Discipline your kids according to their behavior, not the behavior of all the other knuckleheads surfing the Internet.

(‹‹ ›)

Sometimes you'll be fortunate enough to be a virtual parent. Other times you will be forced to be a virtual tyrant. You certainly don't want to upset your children if you don't have to, but if you need to discipline them to protect their well-being and that of your family, don't hesitate for even one moment. Use all means necessary to protect your family. Most of the time, this will include monitoring your kids and installing software that will help you do that. In a few rare and extreme cases, it may mean dropping their laptops into the deep end of the pool.

You are the parent, and you have been empowered by God to raise your children. Don't leave this tremendous responsibility up to the media, the culture, or the next-door neighbor. Be actively involved in your teens' lives, and when you are faced with a difficult situation, remember to be patient, honest, and firm with your kids.

Above all, remember that your job is not to make your kids happy—it is to make them holy.

PART II:

Priorities

4

Sherlock Homes
Tracking the Virtual Footprints

But as for me and my house, we will serve the LORD.
JOSHUA 24:15 NASB

IN *THE MERCHANT OF VENICE,* my good buddy, Bill Shakespeare—known to most people as William—noted, "It is a wise father that knows his own child." Unfortunately, many parents don't know their teens nearly as well as they think they do. One of the reasons so many parents have been outraged by the MySpace phenomenon is that they are hearing about their own children's strange hobbies, unhealthy addictions, and unruly behavior for the first time through others. Their innocent little girl is not as innocent as they thought, and their precious baby boy can hardly be considered precious with the screen name The Groin Ranger.

Fortunately, MySpace is an environment where parents can quickly get caught up on their children's lives and can be involved to whatever degree they desire. Instead of just hearing about your children from the neighbors or Dr. Phil, try walking a mile in your kids' shoes. The best way to get to know your teens is to walk with them, even if their strides are measured in megabytes.

Before you pull out your magnifying glass, let me remind you that we don't need to be Sherlock Holmes to follow our kids—we just need to have Sherlock homes. We don't need a degree in private investigation to know what our teens are doing online. We just need to be interested and involved in all aspects of their lives. Despite what Hillary Clinton may think, it doesn't take a village to raise a godly child. It just takes the love, direction, and full commitment of at least one godly parent.

I can't tell you everything you need to know about teenagers and the struggles they face—you have to be intimately involved in order to gain this insight. I recently spoke in a middle school and a high school about sex, abstinence, and online pressures students face in their personal relationships. I spoke to about 750 kids in a little more than two hours. Later that evening, the sponsor held a similar event for the parents. Ten parents showed up. Out of 750 kids, only ten parents took advantage of the opportunity to gain free insights, get free food, and fellowship with other parents. Understand that if you don't care enough to invest in your teenager's life, you don't have the right to complain. If you aren't going to take the time to raise your son or daughter, don't be upset when MTV or MySpace does.

After reading this book, you will know how to interact with your child online. Even if you are technologically challenged, you will be able to surf the pages of MySpace after walking through this step-by-step tutorial. We'll make sure you are comfortable with the basics of MySpace. The degree to which you are involved in this online community will depend on your children's involvement and your perceived need to monitor them. In this chapter, we are going to make sure that you are well-equipped to navigate this community. In other words, we are going to assist you in helping your children keep their priorities straight.

Becoming a Virtual Parent

I debated about whether or not to have you open your own account at the beginning of this chapter. You certainly don't have to open an account to look at your kid's profile, but I highly recommend that you take a few minutes and open a free account so that you have access to all the communication tools that are available in this virtual schoolyard. If we are trying to do all we can to understand our kids, having our own account is the best option. Having an account will allow you to experience everything your teen does as far as navigating the site, such as receiving and sending e-mail, uploading pictures, writing and receiving blogs.

In order to open an account, go to www.myspace.com. This is the MySpace home page where all 100 million members log on. The home page will usually have some advertisements about a new movie, an up-and-coming band, a crazy video, and some cool new user profiles. If you feel as if you just stepped into the Internet version of the Wild, Wild West, you are probably on the right site.

When you're surfing MySpace, the advertising will quickly catch your eye. It's often very sexual or suggestive. Many dating sites advertise on MySpace with half-naked women and slogans such as "Hot or Not," "It's Nice to Be Naughty," or "Kiss Her or Diss Her?" Unfortunately, this is one aspect of MySpace that the user cannot control. You either have to ignore it, deal with it, or quit visiting the site altogether. I have heard rumors that MySpace will be upgrading the advertising because of the community's increasing popularity and the acquisition by News Corp., but as of January 2007, not much has changed.

On the right side of the page, find the bright orange button that says, SIGN UP! Once you click on this, the simple three-step account-opening process will begin.

Account-Opening Process

1. On the first page that is displayed in the account-opening process, you will have to register as a free user by entering some personal information. Even though MySpace requests certain information, you really only have to give a valid e-mail address and password. The rest of the personal and demographic information does not have to be accurate to open an account.

2. The second page that is displayed will allow you to upload photos so that other users can see who you are. I would

suggest uploading a photo to your account, but if you choose not to, you can always do it later. Any picture of you—even if it is not your "modeling" shot—helps legitimize the account.

3. The third and final page allows you to invite other people to join you in the MySpace community. If you so desire, you can enter your friend's or children's e-mail accounts in the To section, and they will be sent an e-mail alerting them that you joined MySpace. If they know you are on MySpace, they can add you as a friend or visit your page whenever they please.

Once you finish these three basic steps, you will be taken to your own personal home page. This is the page you will see every time you log on to your account. On the left side of the page, about halfway down, there will be a box, outlined in red, with the phrase, Pick your MySpace name/URL! URL stands for Uniform Resource Locator, which simply means it is the file's specified location on the Internet. You can navigate directly to any page you would like by simply typing the Web address into your search engine. Click on the Click Here portion of the box, and you'll be able to pick a unique URL for the profile you just created. In the MySpace world, every address starts with www.myspace.com/. After the slash, you can determine what phrase, name, or signature you want to be remembered by. For example, my personal home page is www.myspace.com/jasonillian. Your teens have specific signatures or call signs they have for their accounts as well. Once you pick a URL, you can't change it, so make sure you pick something you can live with.

After choosing a URL, you will be asked to enter your real name for search purposes. You can enter it if you want other users to be able to search for you by your real name, or you can leave it blank. It is totally up to you. If you like, you can skip this step, and after you have familiarized yourself with MySpace, you can decide whether you want your name floating around.

Mounting the Mouse

Although your desktop mouse may not be as valiant a steed as Seabiscuit, with a few simple clicks, it can quickly carry you into the MySpace community.

To help us learn how to navigate the environment, we are going to examine my own personal account, which you can find at www.myspace.com/jasonillian. If you have already opened your own account, log on and then go to my home page by entering my URL in the Search Web window. If you haven't opened your own personal account, just know that some of the links will not be available to you until you do become a member.

At the top of every page in·the MySpace community, you will see this navigation bar:

Home | Browse | Search | Invite | Film | Mail | Blog | Favorites | Forum | Groups | Events | Videos | Music | Comedy | Classifieds

This navigation bar can take you almost anywhere and can show you almost anything in the community. So, without further ado, let's learn its basic functions.

Home. This link will take you back to the MySpace home page. If you are logged on as a MySpace member, this link takes you back to your own account.

Browse. This link allows you to surf for other MySpace members with either a basic or advanced function. If you want to search for a certain demographic within a 20-mile radius of your home zip code, you can do that here. However, if you are over 18 years old, you cannot search for anyone younger than 18. This is a built-in privacy function to protect teens.

Search. This link is a more specific search tool for locating people. You can search for your teen by his name, display name, or e-mail. In this section, you also have the ability to search for people by their school or affiliated network.

Invite. This link has no function if you are not a member. MySpace members can use this link to invite others onto MySpace by sending them an e-mail.

Film. This link highlights a number of independent movies that are being promoted on MySpace. From time to time, it will also advertise for big Hollywood premiers. To be honest, I don't know very many people who use this function.

Mail. This link allows MySpace members to quickly check their e-mail. If you are not a member, it simply reminds you that you need to sign up if you want to use this function.

Blog. This link is also inactive unless you are a MySpace member. Members can use this link to check their own blogs for new comments and thoughts, and they can also read blogs from any of their friends if they subscribe to their accounts.

Favorites. This link allows members to store certain profiles so they can remember close friends and contacts. It is not available for others to view. People can only use this option if they have created an account with MySpace.

Forum. This link allows both members and nonmembers to view chats in different social circles. If you are not a member of MySpace, you won't be able to post comments in these chat rooms, but you can view the chat threads. From my experience, this area is not as heavily populated or visited as the next link, Groups.

Groups. This link allows members to join certain groups to chat online. Instead of just e-mailing one another or posting comments on everyone's page, members can join groups that discuss specific topics. Many members show which groups they are part of in their profile. Nonmembers can view the chat rooms but cannot participate.

Events. This link allows all users to view real-world events all over the country. This is a growing category where online friends can meet in the real world. Most of the events are parties at clubs, but some events are house parties, movie nights, or other activities. Periodically check this link to see what is going on in your community.

Videos. This is a newer function on MySpace, and it allows users to share, rate, and watch both personal and professional video clips. Unless your child is posting clips of himself or friends online, this will probably not be a concern.

Music. This link allows users to search MySpace for music. MySpace was originally created for independent bands and their fans to share music, track one another, and find concerts. Even though it has grown into more of a social community, MySpace still features cool new artists and promotes music.

Comedy. Comedy is a new link that MySpace just recently added. The original intent of the MySpace community was to promote bands, so the founders thought they could do the same for unknown talent in comedy circles. This link will allow you to search for comedians, watch video clips, and see laugh-out-loud events around the country. The impact of this new link is yet to be determined.

Classifieds. As it suggests, this link is an online classified section for everything from jobs to services to personals. Most teens don't spend much time in this category.

To track your children and see what they are up to online, the three links on the navigation bar that you will want to focus on are Browse, Search, and Groups. Most of the time you'll be able to follow your children around simply by clicking on the different pictures, comments, and blogs on their own pages. To show you how this is done, let's examine my account.

Content and Connections

We briefly discussed this earlier, but I want to reiterate the two main areas of concern that you should be aware of when examining your child's account: content and connections.

Content consists of personal information and identifiable traits that can set your child up for failure. We want our children to have fun, but we don't want them to become targets on the Internet. Most kids are naive about posting their personal information. Because they don't have much life experience, they wrongly assume that everybody is exactly who they say they are and that everyone has good intentions. As you know, this is certainly not the case. MySpace has implemented many layers of warnings and protection, but they cannot possibly monitor everything that gets posted in the community. The MySpace Terms of Use Agreement, which everyone is supposed to read before signing up but few rarely do, includes this statement:

> Please choose carefully the information you post on MySpace.com and that you provide to other Users. Your MySpace.com profile may not include the following items: telephone numbers, street addresses, last names, and any photographs containing nudity, or obscene, lewd, excessively violent, harassing, sexually explicit or otherwise objectionable subject matter. Despite this prohibition, information provided by other MySpace.com Members (for instance, in their Profile) may contain inaccurate, inappropriate, offensive or sexually explicit material, products or services, and MySpace.com assumes no responsibility or liability for this material. If you become aware of misuse of the Services by any person, please contact MySpace or click on the "Report Inappropriate Content" link at the bottom of any MySpace.com page.

As we examine my account, look at all the personal information on my page and decide for yourself if you could easily construct a brief outline of my life and background. Please remember that *I am trying* to make my life transparent so that I can educate young adults on issues of faith and culture. Your kids should not be as open as I have been, even though many teenagers have far more confidential information posted on their pages than I do.

The second area of concern is connections. Our children should not be visiting with unidentified adults and complete strangers on the Internet. The same rule that applies to the real world should apply to the MySpace world: We don't talk to strangers, we don't take candy from them, and we don't get in their cars. To translate to Internet lingo: We don't e-mail with strangers, we don't click on their blogs, links, or imbedded items, and we don't visit their personal pages. Unfortunately, most teens aren't applying these rules. But your kids aren't "most teens," and the standards of Christ aren't negotiable, so we need to thoroughly understand this virtual world to protect your kids.

Monitoring Content and Tracking Connections

When most parents learn of MySpace, they are terrified. They imagine a virtual purgatory where things appear and disappear and where bad men snatch up unsuspecting children. But as you will soon see, it is not nearly that mysterious or complicated. All accounts start with a basic format, and most users just alter the aesthetics of the page to reflect their personalities. Some computer wizards and teen geniuses will take the time to change the layout of their pages, but even when they do, the accounts are still very easy to navigate. If you can click your mouse and use the scroll bar on the side of the page, you are 90 percent of the way to becoming a MySpace expert.

In the MySpace world, everyone wants to be in your Top 8. To be in somebody's Top 8 means that you are one of their top eight friends; therefore, your profile gets prominently displayed on their front page. In honor of this prestigious award—I use the word "prestigious" loosely, of course, because after reviewing certain teens' pages, I'm not sure being associated with them is an honor—I've created the Top 8 ways to monitor your children's content and track their connections. After speaking to numerous MySpace users and visiting with virtual parents, I think I have compiled a very powerful yet user-friendly method for sniffing out virtual footprints. If you want to get the most out of this section, I would suggest reviewing my personal MySpace page during or after each point to make sure you are familiar with the navigation. As you will see, the Top 8 are listed in the order they appear on the page, top to bottom, left to right. The pictures associated with each section will expedite your learning process as well.

Review the Headline Section

As the old adage suggests, a picture is worth a thousand words. This couldn't be more true than it is on MySpace. The first thing you see—the Headline section of a person's page—shouts volumes about how a person sees himself. The entire page reflects a person's creativity, confidence, transparency, and insight, but the headline section is a quick snapshot of his personality and demeanor.

Most people don't join online communities just because they want to be connected. They join because they want to be accepted and valued. They want to know that their opinion matters and that they matter. Many kids don't feel as if they fit in anywhere or have any meaning in their lives, and that is why MySpace is so intriguing. It is a place for them to laugh and joke, flirt and smile, shout and whisper. It is a place for them to try to find themselves. Jesus said, "Come to me, all you who are weary and burdened, and I will give you rest" (Matthew 11:28). But since many kids don't know Him intimately, they are going elsewhere to find rest for their souls. To places like MySpace.

One of the things that makes witnessing so difficult is that in order to speak to someone's heart, you have to know a little bit about his heart's condition. MySpace takes the guesswork out of trying to get to know somebody's heart because much of his life is posted in HTML text for the whole world to see. We just have to know how to read the message between the music and the pictures on each page.

Content

When you first surf to my site, www.myspace.com/jasonillian, you will see that I've decided to go by the screen name "Jason Illian."

Creative, I know. But useful for a speaker and author like myself who wants to brand his message. Users can choose any screen name they can think of, and most people go by a nickname like Babygurl, TrukDvr, or Captain Obvious. Because you want to guard your family's privacy, I would suggest your teens adopt nicknames, or at the very least, use only their first names. If you put your full name on the Internet, it can be searched by anyone, anywhere. There is no real benefit to having your full name on MySpace unless you are trying to market yourself.

Jason Illian

"Somebody slap Paris Hilton for me!"

Male
31 years old
Dallas, TEXAS
United States

Last Login: 10/17/2006

View My: Pics | Videos

Underneath my screen name is a headline title, or tagline. I often put a notable quote like "Somebody slap Paris Hilton for me!" or "Our greatest fear is that we are powerful beyond measure" in this spot to inspire guests and new friends. What a person lists here usually sets the tone for the rest of the page. If you get something suggestive, expect to see scantily clad ladies. If you get something harsh, be prepared to read some angry blogs. A person's tagline often reflects the message on the whole page.

Near the tagline is a small section for personal information such as sex, age, and location. To be honest, I don't know how many people actually tell the truth here. I think more than 50 percent lie about their age, and quite a few people even disguise their actual hometown. A few of my favorites have been "Noneofyourbusinessville" and "Theedgeofnowhere, TX." I think I've actually visited the latter. If you are concerned about predators targeting your daughter, I would suggest that she not disclose her hometown. However, I would suggest having your daughter put her true age. MySpace has safeguards in place to protect the younger users, including limited searches and private profiles. If your daughter lies about her age, she will circumvent all that MySpace is trying to do to protect her. And if something bad were to actually happen, you would want documented proof that your daughter was without fault and telling the truth. Many of the girls who got sexually involved with older guys in the real world lied about their ages on MySpace.

And finally, the picture. Users can upload a number of pictures into the system and rotate the pictures as they see fit. You know the drill here—nothing too revealing, sexy, or flirtatious. If your daughter is 14 years old, don't let her dress like she is 30 and an exotic dancer. You catch what you fish for. If your bait is a girl in her underwear, don't be surprised when you have sexually hungry guys on the line.

Connection

Underneath the pictures in the Headline section of user's profiles are two links: Pics and Videos. Pics is a link that will take you to all the pictures that your teen has uploaded onto the system. Likewise, Videos is a link that will show you all the streaming media videos that your child is sharing on the Internet.

When you click on Pics, you will see that I've uploaded eight to ten pictures, mostly of photo shoots, friends, and family. I try to stay away from posting pictures that are too revealing. Even though I may go for a jog with my shirt off, I'm not sure I want a picture of that floating around for 100 million others to see. I would suggest that you have your teen be equally discreet as well. If you scroll over each picture with your mouse, you can click on it to enlarge it and see other user's comments about it. This is how you see who else is interacting with your child. Each person who leaves a comment also leaves his picture and an electronic footprint to follow. If you click on his picture, you will go directly to his profile. This is how the community stays linked together.

The first time you open the Pics section of your child's site, hold your breath. Many of the parents I've talked to had no idea that certain pictures of their children even existed. We don't live in Polaroid world anymore—we live in cell-phone, digital, easy-to-upload world, and our kids are trading pictures all the time. Fortunately, MySpace has given us a medium to see who they are trading pictures with. If I were you, I'd click on every single person who has left a comment on your child's pictures to review his or her site. When you go to the profile of the person who left the comment, you can see if your child reciprocated and left a comment for him as well. Most of comments on your child's site will probably be from friends and harmless strangers, but it is better to be safe than sorry.

A few things to note when you review your kids' pictures:

- Who is in the pictures with them? If you don't want strangers to piece together their whole lives or know about brothers and sisters, don't allow pictures that show your whole family, close friends, or neighbors.

- What distinguishing landmarks are in the picture? Finding your children is easier if his or her pictures are taken around specific community landmarks. Remove anything that may prove as a navigational beacon for predators.

- What personal information is documented in the picture? Sometimes we take pictures with personal information in the background or on our body. Be aware of this and avoid it when you can.

If you do find some questionable material, don't blow your top. Let's review all the functions of this virtual meeting place first, and then we'll decide how to approach our teens. For now, just know that your kids are making connections, either directly or indirectly, through their pictures.

Browse the General Interest Section

One of the things that draws people to MySpace is the ability to tailor their pages to their own personality. No two pages are the same. Teens are able to personalize each section and share thoughts, pictures, videos, and images with one another.

	Jason Illian's Interests
General	Here are some of my favorite quotes and thoughts:
	"Do not follow where the path may lead. Go instead where there is no path and leave a trail." - Ralph Waldo Emerson
	"I owe my success to having listened respectfully to the very best advice, and then going away and doing the exact opposite." - G. K. Chesterton
	"We must learn to live together as brothers or perish together as fools." - Dr. Martin Luther King, Jr.
	When Alexander the Great visited Diogenes and asked whether he could do anything for the famed teacher, Diogenes replied: 'Only stand out of my light.' Perhaps some day we shall know how to heighten creativity. Until then, one of the best things we can do for creative men and women is to stand out of their light. - John W. Gardner
	"You are so young, my son, and, as the years go by, time will change and even reverse many of your present opinions. Refrain therefore awhile from setting yourself up as judge of the highest matters." - Plato
Music	When I was on ABC's, The Bachelorette, Jay Leno decided to roast me one night on his show for being a virgin. Check it out...it is REALLY funny! I mean, I have to laugh at myself or the pure sexual frustration would drive me insane!
Television	In the following media player, you will find a radio demo for a sex and relationship talk show called, "Undressed", which is being hosted by yours truly and my brother, Guido. It is Loveline-type show that not only addresses relationships but also a number of other issues affecting the 18-35 year old crowd. It has spunk, charisma, and style--at least that is what we are telling ourselves! What you are about to hear was unprepared, unedited, and unrehearsed; some say it is also untalented and uninteresting. However, we have hunted down most of those people. PLEASE NOTE THAT THIS SHOW IS NOT YET ON THE AIR--THE EMAIL ADDRESSES AND PHONE NUMBERS YOU HEAR ARE NOT REAL! Email us your thoughts, email this to your friends, post bulletins about it, write it on a dinner napkin and hand it to your date--whatever you have to do to get the word out. Because being undressed NEVER FELT SO GOOD!
Books	I love to read, and whenever I get a free moment, I try to pick up a new book....here are some of my favorites:
	The Bible, "Mere Christianity" by C.S. Lewis, "Primal Leadership" by Daniel Goleman, "Good to Great" by Jim Collins, "If You Want to Walk on Water, You have to Get Out of the Boat" by John Ortberg, "Messy Spirituality" by Mike Yaconelli. If you have a great recommendation, let me know!
Heroes	Jesus Christ, Martin Luther King, Jr., Mother Teresa, Billy Graham, C.S. Lewis

Of course, this is also part of what can make MySpace dangerous. Some teens don't know what is safe to post and what is not. Because boys long to be viewed as tough, macho men and women long to be viewed as beautiful, sensual women, both sexes have a tendency to post a little too much personal information in the general interest section.

Content

Right underneath the Headline section is the Interests or General Interests section. In my profile, I've taken the liberty to post inspirational quotes, include video and television clips, and expound on my love for music and books. MySpace has default titles such as General, Music, and Television to help users prioritize their different interests, but not all users follow the provided format. A kid can post as little or as much as he wants. He is bound only by his imagination (and, we hope, his parents).

Dozens of websites, such as www.webratsmusic.com and www.blinkyou.com, allow users to post additional information to the General Interest section. Most users have some type of music represented on their site. The type of music and song selection that plays on your children's sites can be indicators of their spiritual health. Of the thousands of sites that I've surfed, I can usually close my eyes and pretty accurately guess the content on the site by the music that plays. If your child has Marylin Manson, Ice Cube, or some other hard-core artist playing, this may be a red flag to feelings of depression or loneliness. Don't ignore it.

I've also learned that teens like to download questionnaires and other surveys that tell more about their likes and dislikes. One of the sites where you can answer a premade questionnaire or customize your own is www.bzoink.com. These can then be pasted on a teen's MySpace account for every king and clown to see. In my opinion, this can be a slippery slope. Nothing is wrong with teens sharing opinions and thoughts with one another, but many of these surveys are personal and sexual in nature. It is one thing to say "My favorite NFL team is the Dallas Cowboys"; it is an entirely different matter when a teen answers, "I've always wanted to experience a threesome."

Please keep in mind that not all the personal information on your teen's site is necessarily true. Kids often say what they think other kids want to hear, which may or may not be the truth. Because some boys feel peer pressure to drink or have sex, they may state that they've had multiple partners and like the taste of Coors. On more than one occasion, I've learned that the boys writing this type of information were not nearly as experienced as they tried to sound. In fact, sometimes the boys had not even kissed a girl. But that doesn't sound cool, so they paint themselves as sex gods.

Whether the information on your child's site is true or not, you can use it as a starting point to reconnect with your teen. Every piece of information can be a talking point, allowing you to discuss delicate and hard-to-initiate issues with your son or daughter. Simply starting to talk about oral sex at the dinner table would be awkward, but if your son answers a survey question about it on his MySpace account, he has opened a door for you to walk through. Believe it or not, many teenagers want to be able to talk to their parents about difficult issues. Most kids don't think their parents would understand or that they would get angry if they broached the subject. But that shouldn't be the case. As parents, we should "be quick to listen, slow to speak and slow to become angry, for man's anger does not bring about the righteous life that God desires" (James 1:19-20).

Connections

In the General Interests section, one of the subtitles that users can display is called Groups. Groups are social circles or virtual chat rooms where MySpace users congregate and discuss particular issues. Hundreds of thousands of groups are associated with MySpace, and teens can join as many as they want. Most of the groups are pretty cheesy and just a waste of time, but on some good ones, users actually discuss topics of abortion, free speech, and the Bible. Groups are organized by categories such as Professional Organizations, Places & Travel, Romance & Relationships, and Entertainment.

Although no specific research is available, most teens seem to join a handful of groups and spend a fraction of their time leaving posts for others to read. For example, one female friend of mine is part of about half a dozen groups, including Risen Magazine, The Flood San Diego,

Friends of Malawi, Mortgage Pros, and Scottsdale Bible Church People. A guy who surfed my site is part of Tri-town Area Pimps, The Bibich Bulldogs Class of 2003, and WWF Raw & Smackdown Fans! Some groups are harmless, and others contain adult discussions and material that a user has to be 18 or older to view.

Though I've chosen not to show my groups, I'm part of a number of them, including The Christian Teens of MySpace, Social Circle, and Undressed: The Naked Truth About Love, Sex, and Dating. If you scroll over a group title on your teen's profile, you will see that you can click on it. Once you click on the title, it will take you directly to the chat group. This is how you can track where your teen is going and who he is interacting with. Most people join groups because they want to leave comments for others to see. Discussions naturally evolve when someone brings up an interesting or controversial topic. As you will see, these groups are easy to navigate, and you can follow your teens' electronic footprints throughout the groups whenever they leave a comment. If people respond to them in the chat room, you can view their profile as well by clicking on their pictures. When people really hit it off in a public chat room, they usually add one another as friends and take the discussion to their personal pages. These interactions create an interwoven social network for teens to navigate as they please.

Like most functions on MySpace, groups are not necessarily good or bad—they are simply communication tools that can be used for good or bad. I suggest that you review the groups in which your teens are participating in order to learn what connections they are making on the Internet. Group titles will tell you much of what the chat room is discussing. If your teens don't post their groups for others to see on their profile pages—and, like me, many teens don't even though they are part of numerous groups—you may have to ask. If they hesitate to tell you where they are involved, this is usually a sign that they don't want you to know. When I was growing up, I usually stalled with my parents when they were on to me about hanging out with the wrong kids or staying up too late.

Today's teens do the same thing, but now the battle has shifted to the Internet.

Read the Personal Details Section

In the last two or three sections on the left side of the page, you should see some boxes that say, Jason Illian's Details, Jason Illian's Schools, and Jason Illian's Companies. These areas combine to make up the Personal Details section of your children's accounts. This information may be quite useful for adults looking to network or track old friends, but most of the information in these categories is detrimental to your teens. Information in these categories include hometown, body type, schools attending or attended, and companies or networking. The only way I would allow teens under my supervision to state their hometown and school on their MySpace accounts was if they set their profiles to private (which I will teach you how to do in the next chapter) and if they agreed not to let strangers see their accounts. In most other circumstances, I can't see the benefit of having personal information floating around this online community.

Jason Illian's Interests	
Status:	In a Relationship
Here for:	Friends
Orientation:	Straight
Hometown:	Lake Havasu City, AZ
Body type:	6' 4" / Athletic
Ethnicity:	White / Caucasian
Religion:	Christian - other
Zodiax Sign:	Virgo
Smoke / Drink:	No / No
Children:	Someday
Education:	College graduate
Occupation:	Author / Speaker

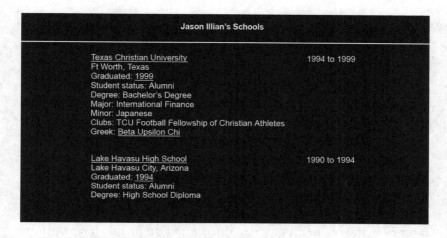

Content

"The problems of the offline world are the same problems of the online world," says CEO and cofounder of MySpace, Chris DeWolfe. "When you grow up, the first thing your parents teach you is to look both ways before you cross the street and to not get in cars with strangers. It is very similar for the Internet."[1] Kids could have prevented many of the issues they have had with MySpace by taking the precautions they normally would in the brick-and-mortar world. This starts by stripping their profiles of any revealing information.

Kids should avoid (or be very careful with) a few basic information questions in this section. First is Status. If your teenage girl answers this question, she only has five options: In a Relationship, Single, Divorced, Married, or Swinger. As you can imagine, if she answers Single or Swinger, she is going to be (virtually) approached by many eager guys. Of course, Swinger shouldn't be an option, but since we live in a very confused society, I'm not surprised that it is. Many of my single, Christian, female friends show they are In a Relationship on their profile to avoid being bothered by guys who may or may not have good intentions. But even if your daughter opts for In a Relationship, she may still be approached by guys. Before I married my wife, she was contacted by many strange, single guys even though her profile clearly noted, "In a Relationship."

The next question about sexual Orientation goes hand-in-hand. A user's only options are Bi, Gay/Lesbian, Straight, No Answer, and Not Sure. If you wonder if you have just spiraled into the seventh layer of hell, you are not alone. Since when do people have options on their sexuality? But before you throw your computer out the window, let's think about this question for a moment. As Christians, we know that "God created man in his own image" (Genesis 1:27) and that the only option should be Straight. However, we live in a fallen world, and many teens are confused about sexual orientation. Since we can't lock our teens in closets until they are adults, we can use this ridiculous question as a teaching moment. Your teens will probably answer Straight, in which case you can breathe a sigh of relief. But some teens—or their friends—may answer in other ways, and you'll have to deal with the issue. Whatever you do, don't lose your temper over this, regardless of how they have answered! Wait until you have prayed about it and collected your thoughts before discussing it with your teens.

Many parents are surprised when they log on to their child's account and see that little Jimmy answered Yes to Smoke/Drink. This is something you hope your teen never indulges in, but knowing that it is happening is better than living in ignorance. At least you can do something about it. Likewise in regards to the question about Religion. Just because little Jimmy has been going to church for the last 14 years doesn't make him a Christian, and he may make that obvious on his profile. If he does, you have more information that will motivate you to pray and reach out to him.

When all is said and done, the most important thing you need to protect is your children's location so that stalkers and sexual predators can't find them. Two profile questions—Hometown and School Name—are dead giveaways for anybody searching MySpace. Unless your teens' profiles are set to private and you thoroughly trust them not to change them, do not let your kids list their school or hometown. Their close friends will be able to find them by a name or e-mail search. Your kids don't need their hometown or school listed on their accounts. If I were a sexual predator, the first thing I would do would be to search the nearest zip code for young girls in the area. Once I had a list of them, I would review their profiles to see which schools they attend. If neither bit of information is on your kids' accounts, stalkers will be less likely to take their addiction from the click world to the brick world.

Connections

Most of your concern in the Personal Details section should be about content, not connections. Unless an Internet wizard greatly alters his page format, the only place your teens can connect to others in this section is through their schools. If you allow your teenage girl to enter her school, you may be able to link to a page that searches for others who are attending or have attended her school. But remember, if you can pull up your daughter's friends from her school link, predators can do it as well. And the reverse is also true. If a stranger stumbles upon one of your daughter's friends' accounts, he'll be able to find your daughter through her school link.

For example, if you run your mouse over Texas Christian University on my personal page, you can link to a list of other people who attended TCU. This is a convenient function, but it may not be the safest thing for middle- or high-school students.

Read Your Teen's Blogs

Parents often tell me that they wish they knew what their kids were thinking. After surfing MySpace for a year and reading hundreds of blogs, my response is, "Be careful what you ask for!"

Many kids are telling the world *exactly* what they think in their blogs. In its simplest form, a blog—short for "Web log"—is a personal online journal that is intended for public consumption. Think of it as a diary that you share with 100 million of your closest friends. And it is the latest fad on social networking sites such as MySpace. Some people blog to share their opinions on political events, to creatively express their artistic abilities, to be poetic or entertaining, to express their feelings, or just to get their problems off their chest. Because of the popularity of MySpace and its easy navigation, if someone writes a powerful blog, thousands of people can read it in a matter of hours. It is a way for teens to express themselves.

But some kids are expressing themselves in ways that do more harm than good. In June 2006, a 14-year-old suburban Chicago teenager threatened the life of a school official on his MySpace blog. He was later charged for felony harassment.[2] On another unrelated blog, a 16-year-old girl talks about her 18-year-old boyfriend and about how she has been to bed with him. Another 16-year-old writes this on her page:

> It's mostly late at night when I should be sleeping that all my frustrations and irrational fears come to the surface. I have all these things lurking deep in my mind and I don't know what to do with them.
>
> I still have insecurities about my looks. I don't understand why I have some days where I like the way I look, but most of the time I hate everything about my face and my body.[3]

And these few examples are just the tip of the iceberg. Kids talk about homework, relationships, drinking, sports, movies, friends— you name it! Even though MySpace has a feature that can block anyone except preapproved friends from seeing a blog, very few teenagers use it. Most blogs are visible for the whole World Wide Web to see. So if a father really wants to know what his son is thinking, the best thing to do is to talk to him…and if that doesn't work, read his blog.

Content

Blogging can be a good and healthy thing if it is used correctly. Since most teens are somewhat restricted on where they can go and what they can do—it's called "good parenting"—teens often reach out to their peers for advice on things like dating and pursuing their dreams. Most parents err on being overly cautious and realistic when raising their kids. They want to protect their teens. They don't want to see them fail. This is an admirable parenting strategy, but we have to remember that kids also need to dream and use their God-given imagination. Parents should help their kids strike a delicate balance between keeping their feet on the ground and their heads in the clouds. Blogging can be an outlet for this creativity if boundaries are in place.

Parents need to monitor two types of content in the virtual world:

Personal information. Personal information includes things such as names, addresses, phone numbers, e-mail, and names of schools. If this type of information leaks out, strangers may be able to *physically* touch your daughter's life. According to a recent study done by Children's Digital Media Center at Georgetown University, two-thirds of teen bloggers include their ages and at least their first names. Nearly a quarter of bloggers include their full names.[4]

Private information. Private information includes things such as dating relationships, sexual histories, addictions, tragic family stories, and fragile dreams. If this type of information leaks out, strangers may be able to *emotionally* and *spiritually* touch your daughter's life. Some teens think just because they don't post personal information such as their home address, other MySpace users can't touch them. This is far from the truth. The things we share from the depths of our hearts are far more likely to scar us than our physical experiences. And these things can quickly be disseminated all over the Internet.

A few parents have told me that their teens often shut down the computer, switch pages, or wait for them to leave the room before they will continue blogging on MySpace. Their teens argue that they deserve to have privacy, and the parents often give it to them. But if they want privacy, why are they writing on MySpace? MySpace is in the public domain and is free to anyone who can connect to the Internet. If your teens want to express their thoughts in complete privacy, they need to start their own diaries, not blog in a virtual community. Besides, as we mentioned earlier, your house in not a democracy. When your teens pay their own bills, buy their own houses, and have their own jobs, they can vote on their Internet rules. Until then, they have to play by yours.

Some kids will quickly concede to an open-computer policy where you can look over their shoulder at any time, and other kids will battle you every step of the way. Each situation is unique, and you need to prayerfully discern how much freedom to give your kids. As your teens get older and prepare to leave the nest, I would suggest slowly granting them more and more responsibility on things such as MySpace (if you deem them worthy). Someday you won't be there to protect them anymore, and you want them to respect you enough to continue coming to you for advice.

Regardless of how things shake out, "always be prepared to give an answer to [your son when he] asks you to give the reason for the hope that you have. But do this with *gentleness* and *respect*" (1 Peter 3:15-16). If you always convey gentleness and respect, you will build bridges between you and your children that they can walk across anytime they need you.

Connections

If you look at my page, you will see the titles of a number of blogs. If you navigate to one of these articles, you will be able to read my thoughts and ramblings on these subjects.

Underneath each one of the articles, you may find comments from different friends and MySpace comrades. You can check out people who have commented on my articles simply by clicking on their pictures. This will take you directly to their personal pages. I would suggest that you not only go to your teens' pages and read all their blogs, but that you also review all the comments from their friends as well. If people have commented on your kids' pages, your kids have probably commented on their pages as well. In reciprocal friendships, MySpace buddies often support one another's writings and thoughts.

If your child has written something that is questionable or outright unacceptable, make sure to see who has commented and supported his thoughts. Don't hesitate to navigate to another person's page and see what his outlook on life is. You need and deserve to know who is influencing your child's life, because at the end of the day, you are responsible to the Lord for your child's upbringing.

Bounce Through the Blurbs

Right underneath the list of blogs, my profile page has a section called Jason Illian's Blurbs that has two primary areas: About Me and Who I'd Like to Meet. I've included a paragraph about my life and career with a photo slide show. In the About Me section, I've followed it up with a couple short paragraphs about passionate people in the Who I'd Like to Meet portion. There is also a link to my personal website if you scroll over the bold phrase, "Check out Jason Illian.com for more relationship stuff." And from time to time, I also include small banners promoting my books and speaking tours.

Much like the rest of the page, each section can be tailored to a person's own desires and personality. Many teens check their MySpace accounts multiple times a day because things are always changing and evolving. No generation has been as connected, dynamic, or open as today's teens, as you can see on their pages. If a teen girl wants to impress a young guy, she can quickly log on to her account and put his name in the Who I'd Like to Meet section.

Likewise, a young stud can reword his About Me section if he knows the girl of his dreams likes guitar players.

Content

The information shared in these two sections is usually not as thorough as the thoughts written in a blog, but it is more prominently displayed on the front of a person's page. People who really want to get to know you will check out your blogs, but most people will simply skim over the front page of your profile to learn about your habits and interests. This is why the content in this area is so important.

When I navigate to a new person's page, the first thing I notice is the Headline section, and the second thing I notice are the blurbs. Many kids have short attention spans, and if they don't see something that catches their attention in the first 15 seconds, they will surf to another page. With 100 million users on MySpace, you don't need to hang out on a page that doesn't interest you.

I may sound like a broken record (or maybe I should say a damaged MP3), but review the blurbs on your children's profiles and make sure they are not displaying any personal or private information. If your son is creative and wants to express his personality, good for him, but don't let him be so creative that he attracts every thug, prostitute, and stalker in a 100-mile radius. Our kids may feel like adults, but they are still kids, and they need guidance when operating in a virtual world without boundaries.

Connections

In most profiles, the blurbs include a few connections or links. But more technically advanced pages may include hidden links that allow you to jump to another Web page with just a flick of the wrist. On my page, for example, a user can link to my personal Web page, www.jasonillian.com, by simply clicking on Check out Jason Illian.com for more relationship stuff. Roll your mouse over anything in your child's blurbs that may contain a hidden link. If you find pictures of scantily clad girls or questionable paraphanilia, certainly try to click on those pictures. Many times these pictures are actually hidden links that navigate the user out of MySpace to other parts of the Internet. Sexually explicit images and pornography are not allowed in MySpace, but users can link to it from places in MySpace. Make sure those things don't exist on your kids' profiles or on their friends' profiles.

Review the Top 8

One of the best ways to find out what your teen is doing is to figure out who he is hanging out with. Reviewing your son's best friends will tell you more about his health than a CAT scan at the local children's hospital.

If you asked your son to write down his top eight friends, as well as his likes in music, girls, and passions, he would most likely blow you off. Very rarely do teens want to expose their best friends because in reality, they know they would be exposing themselves. But this is exactly what you are able to learn by reviewing your son's Top 8 friends on MySpace. A person's Top 8 are the eight friend profiles prominently displayed on a user's front page. Users can display their top 12, 16, or 24 friends, but many people stick to the default Top 8 format.

As I'm writing this, my first three profiles are of Alisha (my wife), Josh Cox (my good buddy), and Ben (my brother). I usually rotate the other five profiles so that I don't unintentionally hurt any of my friends' feelings. (Who would have guessed that having friends could be so much work?) Consciously or not, most users put people they are close to in their Top 8. And teens can get themselves in big relationship trouble if they don't have their significant other in the coveted number one position.

I'm telling you, the Top 8 provides a plethora of information on your kids. By reviewing their closest friends, you can figure out who they are hanging out with, what type of music they listen to, who they are dating, what styles are cool, what movies they want to see, where the big parties are, and much more. You couldn't dig up this much information on your teen's personal life if you had the gestapo interrogate him for a month!

Of course, this is exactly why it can be dangerous to your kids as well. You can't police all of their friends' sites, but by making sure your teens aren't sharing too much personal information, you can make sure the electronic footprints don't lead back to your house should something go wrong in this virtual community.

Content

At the top of the Friend Space, you will see how many friends your child has accumulated. In my profile, as of this writing, I have

1534 "close" friends. I say this jokingly, of course, because having thousands of close friends is impossible. Truth be told, of all the people on my list, I only personally know about a hundred of them. The others are people I have interacted with on MySpace and who enjoy reading my material. Unless your daughter has a career in the public eye, you should be wary if she has thousands of friends. This is usually a red flag.

A great question to ask your teens when reviewing the material on their pages and their friends' pages is, why? Why do you have these pictures on your page? Why did you accept that half-naked drummer as a friend? Why do you talk about drinking in your profile? Why? Many kids do things because they can. Very rarely do they stop and ask themselves why they are doing them. Don't ask in a condescending or demeaning way, but ask so that they know you are legitimately trying to understand their perspective. Many teenagers will remove trashy material from their site once they know their parents are concerned. They want their parents' approval.

In the waters of MySpace, you catch what you fish for. The type of content you show on your page will determine the type of people who request to be your friend. If you show lots of skin and talk about sex, you'll attract testosterone-driven males and playboy-type females. If you talk about drugs and guns, you'll attract NRA and gang members. If you talk about God and faith, you'll attract Christians. If we can remind teens that their profiles don't exist in a vacuum and that anyone can view their pages, we will empower them to make wise decisions. Then their pages will more likely reflect their true hearts.

Connections

At the bottom of my Friend Space, you can View All of Jason Illian's Friends. When you click on this link, you will feel as if you're getting sucked into a parallel universe. On the following pages, you will be able to see *all* of my 1534 (and counting) so-called friends.

Every profile, every picture, and every comment will be at your fingertips. Here is where your investigative skills must kick in.

If you want to know who your son has been corresponding with over the Internet, you can follow his electronic footprints across his Friend Space. He either invited or allowed everybody on that list to be his friend—why? That is what you have to find out. Hopefully, you'll open up his list and find only his close basketball buddies from school and his Bible study group from church. But if your child is like most teenagers, at least a couple questionable characters will be on his list. Your job is to determine which ones are questionable and which ones are legitimate.

The first thing you want to do is review all his Top 8 friends. They are in his Top 8 for a reason, and if you don't know what that reason is, you need to keep digging. The good (and bad) thing about MySpace is that teens aren't trying to hide anything. In fact, they are often quite flamboyant in their actions and speech. So you shouldn't have too much trouble figuring out why his Top 8 friends are his Top 8 friends. If something shady is going on, you will probably notice it quickly. A 27-year-old female in a string bikini in your teenage son's Top 8 should set off a parenting alarm.

After reviewing the Top 8, take a brief look at all of his other friends. If your child has accumulated hundreds or thousands of friends, this could be a bit cumbersome. Most parents don't have an unlimited amount of time to review each page, so just review the pictures and the screen names to decide who to investigate further. Screen names like "JesusRulz" and "How Bout Them Lakers?" are probably not a concern. But names like "SexiBlondi" and "SINglenLookin" probably deserve another look. Even if they turn out not to be questionable characters, at least you will have educated yourself on some of the things that are happening in the teenage world.

Examining your son's friends is the best way to follow him around MySpace. His friends can leave comments on his pictures, be part of his friends list, and leave comments on his front page. By examining the profiles of his friends and his friends' friends, you will quickly see that six degrees of separation closes down fast in MySpace.

Read the Comment Section

The last section we have to review is the Friend's Comments section at the bottom right-hand side of the page. A user's preapproved friends are the only ones who can leave messages in this section. The Comments portion of MySpace is a hybrid between e-mail and a billboard. A friend can leave a note for everyone to read as well as imbedded images, links, and pictures.

Many people make new friends by seeing someone in another person's Top 8 or reading an inspiring comment someone left on a person's page. I've learned that if a person leaves a comment on your page, you feel obligated to return the favor by leaving a message on that person's page as well. Of course, this type of reciprocal correspondence can greatly help you track your kids. If someone has left multiple comments on your child's front page, click on that user's profile and you will probably see multiple comments from your kid on his page as well. Although MySpace has no formal rules about proper correspondence, most people try to reach out to those people who have reached out to them.

Content

Content is not a big concern in the Top 8 section, but parents should monitor it in the Comment section. With more than 100 million members in the community, many people are trying to get attention, and they often do so by leaving messages and images in other people's comment boxes. If you look at my profile, you'll see that the front page alone includes about 50 comments from various people, some merely with text and others with text and pictures. If you don't set up your account to preapprove the comments before they show on your page, you may have pictures of half-naked women displayed on your own profile without your permission.[5] When I first set up my account, I was naive enough to believe that people would act with integrity and character. I learned the hard way when I logged on one afternoon to see a giant rear end and a G-string staring me in the face.

Even though only a maximum of 50 comments can be included on a person's home page, you can view all the comments that users have left on your child's account simply by clicking the View All link at the top of the comment box. Much like an e-mail inbox, the older comments will continue to be stored until the profile owner discards them. And although a visitor can't erase or block any comments on a friend's site, the account creator can remove any of them at any time.

The Comment section is probably the most innovative tool that MySpace has provided to link users together. It is interesting to look at a friend's account and see who else is connected to your good buddy or girlfriend. I've reconnected with old friends, stayed in touch with family members, and even started business deals through comments I've found on different sites. But you have to be careful not to act unruly or stupid when leaving comments for a friend. Once you post a sentence or an image, you can't take it back. Some adults have learned this the hard way. Certain firms are searching MySpace before hiring, and many people are getting turned down because of their behavior online.

Although it can be challenging, try to teach your children to be discerning when posting information on someone else's page. Remind them not to post anything they don't want shared with 100 million other people at the click of the mouse.

Connections

After reviewing the profiles of your daughter's Top 8 friends, I would recommend reviewing the profiles of those people who have left comments on her site. Many kids have hundreds of friends, and instead of wasting time rummaging through all of them, you can probably figure out who she is talking to 80 percent of the time by reviewing the profiles of the people in her Comment section.

The real power of MySpace is that people can put a face with their thoughts in the Comment section. E-mail is great, but sometimes we don't know who we are talking to on the other side. MySpace gives the appearance of a real person with real feelings and a real body on the other side. Of course, as you will see later in the book, appearances can be deceiving.

I can't tell you how many people have come to my site because they read something about me in another person's Comment section. Teens share friends like celebrities gossip, and information gets around quickly in MySpace. In larger cities, teens are able to connect with people at other schools. In smaller towns, teens are able to reach out and meet people in other cities. The entire dynamic of growing up has changed. Kids have accelerated their maturation process. As parents, we need to make sure that they are able to decipher all this new information correctly, weed through the spam and junk, make decisions based on their Christian values, and act accordingly. But we should be doing that anyway. MySpace is just forcing us to start communicating with kids about deeper issues at an earlier age.

Try not to think of the virtual friend-making process as a bad thing. Think of each good connection as a blessing and each bad connection as a teachable moment. Masses of hurting and lost people are undoubtedly participating on MySpace every day. Many of them are reaching out for somebody—anybody!—to be their friend. They often reach out in vain, trying to be popular by selling sex, drugs, and rock 'n' roll, but we should be thankful they are reaching out at all. When Jesus saw the large crowds following Him—many of whom were completely lost—"he had compassion on them and healed their sick" (Matthew 14:14). As believers, we need to have compassion on those who are lost, and we've been given a unique opportunity in this virtual community to teach our children to do the same. If our teens learn how to navigate these rough waters now, they will be much better prepared to take on more issues later in life.

Surf Your Teen's Entire Profile

If you have taken the time to walk through the last seven steps, you know the basics for navigating your child's MySpace page. The last thing you need to do is to run your mouse over any pictures, comments, banners, and images on her page to see if anything has a hidden link. From time to time, you'll find certain phrases and pictures with imbedded links that catapult you to another Internet page. Some are harmless; others are not. Check the entire profile just to be sure.

《《 》》

Many teenagers display unsatisfied curiosity. They will ask, seek, and knock until a door is opened for them. As parents, we need to imitate this youthful exuberance and curiosity by diving headfirst into the digital world. Don't be afraid to make mistakes or stumble onto the wrong Web pages. We all get lost and confused the first couple of times we try something new. You don't have to spend an hour surfing the virtual waves every day, but take a couple minutes every other day to learn something new about MySpace. Use the top eight steps that I've taught you as a starting point. You'll be surprised how quickly you pick it up.

Most importantly, remember why you are doing all of this—to stay connected and intimately involved in your children's lives. If being part of an online community feels awkward or odd for you, imagine how odd it must have felt for Christ to go from heaven to earth. We all make sacrifices for those we love.

5

Souls Without Soles

Teaching Our Children Not to Leave Footprints

Above all else, guard your heart,
for it is the wellspring of life.
PROVERBS 4:23

IN THE LAST CHAPTER, WE learned how to create Sherlock homes. We discussed the basics about navigating MySpace, viewing your children's accounts, and understanding the principles that make this community so addictive and exciting. We also learned how to follow your kids around this virtual maze. In this chapter, we are going to build on your new knowledge and help you cover your children's electronic footprints so that others can't see all their blogs, meet all their friends, and find them in the real world. We are going to make sure that their souls don't have soles—that they leave no tracks.

If you are like the myriad of other parents I've spoken to, you are probably still a little hesitant and skeptical of this whole MySpace thing. Something deep inside you wants to toss the PC out the second-story window and revert back to good ol' face-to-face communication. I understand. I really do. A little bit of resistance to change can be a good thing. When dealing with a communication tool where people can lie, deceive, and seduce, we should approach with caution, taking one step at a time. But avoiding this topic completely or putting a ban on your child's Internet communication isn't the answer either. We need to find a healthy balance.

In John 17:15, Jesus prayed, "My prayer is not that you take them out of the world but that you protect them from the evil one."

God's wisdom is mysterious, isn't it? Although He had the power to take His children out of the world, He didn't do so. In fact, Jesus didn't even pray that God would do so. Instead, He prayed that God would protect them from the evil one exactly where they were. Yet parents are often quick to remove their children from danger instead of equipping them for the battle. The online world can be a dangerous place, but if you think about it, so can the real world. Instead of removing children from all danger—which is virtually impossible, and which leaves them defenseless when they do face problems—we need to properly equip them for the battle. And then pray God will protect them.

I'm passionate about tackling the MySpace phenomenon because I've seen the emotional damage teenagers suffer when they have no guidance, direction, or love in their lives. Many of the teenagers I've met over the years have become like little brothers and sisters to me, and I want God to empower them to "act justly and to love mercy and to walk humbly with [their] God" (Micah 6:8). But the battle for their souls has become more vicious than ever, and I've learned that parents *must* be involved in their development if they want them to be Christlike.

The media may lead you to believe that MySpace doesn't care about the safety of your children, but I think their nonchalant stance has been grossly exaggerated. Don't get me wrong, MySpace is concerned about making money and building a powerful company, but they also want to make sure that your kids are safe from freaks, geeks, and strangers. But at the end of the day, *nobody* cares about your children as much as you do, and you can't rely on anybody but yourself (and God, of course) to protect your children. God will ultimately hold you responsible for their growth, so don't underestimate the exceptionally important role that you play.

I've been chillin' in the MySpace world for about a year, and in that time, I've documented the five best ways to help teens cover their tracks in this community. If you can get your arms around these strategies, you'll have built immeasurably helpful defenses around your kids.

Go Stealth

Probably the best way to protect your children is to suggest that they make their profiles private so only friends can see them. All users have the option of making their profiles private, but if a user is younger than 16 and creates an account with her correct birth date, her account is automatically private. In other words, if your child is 14 or 15 and is honest about her age, her account is set by default to be viewable only to MySpace members on her friends list. If your teen would like, she can make it visible to anyone under the age of 18 on MySpace, but the general public cannot see it. Adults who are 18 or older cannot send an e-mail to a 14- or 15-year-old, nor can they request to be added as friends unless they know the teenager's last name or valid e-mail address. This is a valuable security feature that MySpace has added to help protect teens.

If your teen has falsified her information to make herself look older, you can help her rectify the situation. To make a profile private, log on to the account, and you will see the home page. From there, click on Edit Profile in the Headline section, go to the Basic Info tab that appears at the top, and then change the birth date. Once the system sees that your child is really 14 or 15 years old, it will make the profile private and take the necessary precautions to protect her.

If your teen is 16 or older, she can still have a private profile without lying about her age. From the home page, click on the Account Settings button, which is next to the profile picture. About a quarter of the way down the page is a link called Privacy Settings. Once you go to that link, you can decide Who Can View My Full Profile. For users 16 or older, the options are My Friends Only or Public. For users younger than 16, the options are My Friends Only or Anyone Under 18 on MySpace. If a 14- or 15-year-old changes the default on her privacy settings so that anyone under 18 on MySpace can view her profile, this message pops up:

> **MySpace is a public space.** Don't post anything you wouldn't want the world to know (e.g. your phone number,

address, instant messenger screen name, or specific where-abouts).

People aren't always who they say they are. Exercise caution when communicating with strangers and avoid meeting people in person whom you do not fully know. If you must meet someone, do it in a public place and bring a friend or trusted adult.

Harassment, hate speech, and inappropriate content should be reported. If you feel someone's behavior is inappropriate, react. Talk with a trusted adult, or report it to MySpace or the authorities.

MySpace is working hard to protect teens, so it is important that parents help them in any way that they can. Don't let your teen lie about her age or status. If she does, she can go around the security measures that MySpace has put in place to protect her.

In my opinion, half of the battle has been won when your teen's profile is private. But remember, her profile is stealthy, not invisible. Other users can still search for your teen by name or e-mail address and can see her profile picture, tag line, gender, age, location, and last log in. But at least the profile is not easily accessible, and personal information, such as pictures, addresses, and blogs, are not visible to the whole world.

Change Privacy Settings

Another strategy you can use in addition to or in place of private profiles is to change your teens' privacy settings. You can make a number of small tweaks to protect your teens' personal and private information.

Once again, go to the Home page of your account and find the Account Settings link. Once you click on this link, you will see another page with a number of different options. About a quarter of the way down the page is a section called Privacy Settings with a link called Change Settings. From this link, you can make a number of powerful adaptations to the account including but not limited to these:

- *Friend requests—require email or last name.* When you check this box, no user can request to be your friend unless they enter your e-mail or last name. This makes interfacing with your kids extremely difficult for strangers. It prevents stalkers and pedophiles from joining your teens' friends list. In order for a stranger to gain access to your child, your child has to approve a friend request. If you have taught him not to talk to strangers, the door is shut.

- *Comments—approve before posting.* When you check this box, your teens will have to approve their friends' comments before allowing them to be posted on your kids' profiles or blogs. If they are crude, obnoxious, or sexual, your teens can just choose to delete them.

- *Hide online now.* This prevents other users from knowing when you are at the computer. If you leave this blank, a little flashing orange spot tells others when you are online.

- *Blog comments—friends only.* This allows only people whom you have accepted as friends to comment on your blogs. If you choose not to protect this, anyone can comment on your blogs, and the comments will be public for others to see.

- *Group invites—friends only.* To protect the younger users, this box will automatically be checked if the member is younger than 18. By checking this box, MySpace can prevent teens from participating in group discussions targeted for mature audiences. In other words, your teen cannot be asked to join a chat room except by friends on his list, and the chat rooms he can join should be rather clean (*should* is the key word).

A few other functions are available under Privacy Settings, but these are the ones that can have the biggest impact on your child's account.

Change Profile Settings

From the same Account Settings area, you can select another function called Profile Settings about three-fourths of the way down the page. Much like the Privacy Settings link, this gives you ability to make a few small changes that affect your teens' groups and comments.

- *Display groups I belong to.* By checking this box, your teen can display all the groups she belongs to. This is not a wise idea! Leave this box unmarked! We are trying to limit the number of ways a stranger could follow her around this virtual roller rink, and if your daughter displays her groups, she is opening up a whole new world for others to explore. Don't give other users the ability to read everything you post, everywhere you post it.

- *Disable HTML…Comments.* You can disable three different types of HTML comments on this link—profile, picture, and blog comments. Just to review, HTML comments are usually images, flash files, sparkle tags, and other nonword-related information that others can post on your page. If your teen decides to approve comments before posting, she is probably okay leaving these sections unchecked. But if you start visiting her profile from time to time and see things such as pictures of half-naked men and crude image files, you may have to ask her to disable her HTML comments.

Edit the Profile

After reviewing your teen's profile, you will probably want her to remove at least a few bits of personal and private information. Most teens who have accounts have been a bit too liberal in posting their stats. Knowing you live in Texas, is one thing; knowing you live in Plano, Texas, and having your exact street address is another matter entirely.

Fortunately, you can quickly change almost everything on MySpace. With a few clicks of the mouse, you can change personal information, such as your daughter's school; private information, such as her medical conditions; or pictures that reveal way too much. Every bit of information that your teen has included on her profile page can be changed from the Edit Profile link on her home page. Once you click on Edit Profile, you will see this navigation bar on your screen:

Interests & Personality | Name | Basic Info | Background & Lifestyle |
Schools | Companies | Networking | Song & Video on Profile

This is a quick reference guide to what information your teen can change in each area. Now you won't be uninformed when you ask her to change her headline (tagline) and she says, "I don't know how to do it."

- *Interests & Personality.* Your teen can edit or change any information in the Headline, About Me, Who I'd Like to Meet, Interests, Music, Movies, Television, Books, and Heroes. She can also change her background and music from this section.

- *Name.* Your teen can change her Display Name and her First and Last Name for search purposes. If you don't want people to search for her by her last name, I suggest you have her change it.

- *Basic Info.* Your teen can change her Gender, Date of Birth, Occupation, City, Country, State/Region, Zip/Postal Code, Ethnicity, Body Type, Height, and I Am Here For, which includes Dating, Serious Relationships, Friends, or Networking.

- *Background & Lifestyle.* Your teen can change her Marital Status, Sexual Orientation, Hometown, Religion, Smoker, Drinker, Children, Education, and Income.

- *Schools.* Your teen can change her school or delete it altogether.

- *Companies.* Your teen can change any Companies that she represents, works for, or supports.

- *Networking.* Your teen can change any Networking which she may do in this category. Most teens don't use this section.

- *Song & Video on Profile.* Your teen can change the Music

on her profile in this section. She may also change it in
the Interests & Personality section if she copied it from
another site.

If you read your daughter's profile and are fuming about what she
has written, take a few moments (or if needed, a few days) to calm
down before addressing the situation. You will neither gain your
daughter's respect nor rectify the situation quickly if she immediately
goes into defense mode. Remember, the whole point of learning
about MySpace is to be intimately involved in her life. If you fly off
the handle about how stupid or naive she is, she will probably do one
of two things: (1) She'll make her profile private and not add you as
a friend so you can't see what she is doing, or (2) she'll completely
ignore you and continue with her online life anyway. You can't access
her account or change one bit of information without her account
name and password. You have to work together!

Clean House

I'd like to say that you will only have to take a fine-toothed comb
to your teens' accounts and straighten up a few little things. But you
stand a good chance of needing a shovel and a big Hefty bag to clean
up all the droppings floating around on their sites. In addition to
removing all personal and private information from planet MySpace,
you may have to sit down and talk to your teens about deleting some
friends and groups with which they have associated themselves.

Notice I didn't say, "Demand that he remove certain hoodlums
from his account immediately," or "Force him to repent or punish
him with beans and franks for a month!" This has to be a collabora-
tive effort, or you will probably be on the losing end. You can punish
him in the real world, but by doing so, you may only inflame the
problem. Many teens who are acting foolishly on MySpace by being
overtly sexual are doing it from their emptiness; they are acting
out so that someone will show them attention and affirmation. If
your teen is doing this, don't take his actions personally or think
you are a bad parent. Consider yourself blessed that this has come

to your attention at a time when you can do something about it. If you handle the situation properly, it can draw the two of you closer together instead of pushing you apart.

If your teen wants to remove certain friends from his account, he can do so from his home page. When he first logs on to his account, he will see a box at the right-hand side of the page called My Friend Space. On the top right corner of that box is a link called Edit Friends. By clicking on this link, he can delete any questionable people from his account. Instead of telling him whom he should delete, ask him if he thinks his account includes anybody whose behavior or speech may reflect poorly on him. Empower him to make the appropriate decision on his own. If he neglects to make a good call, be a little more directive on the second approach with "I think we may need to delete BigHooter Yum-Yum from your account, don't you think?" Use parental power as a last resort.

The same goes for your son's Groups. On the home page, he can click on the Groups link on the toolbar at the top of the page. When his list of personal groups comes up, he'll need to click on the particular group he wishes to delete from his account. Once the group profile is displayed, all he has to do is click on the button labeled Resign on the group's home page. It's that simple—that group will be removed from his personal profile.

Your teen may need to remove other links, banners, and music as well. Your original gut instinct will be to remove everything that even remotely identifies your son or has a hint of culture in it. But be reasonable. Remember, you wouldn't be comfortable watching one of your son's dates from the backseat of his car either, but most parents don't stop their kids from dating. It's part of growing up. If you can find a middle ground with him, he'll still enjoy chatting with friends online, and you'll know more about him than you ever thought possible. Both parties can win.

Guarding Their Hearts

I'm not suggesting that you have to force your teen to implement all these strategies on his or her account. Some teens are mature enough to handle a little bit more freedom, and if your child happens to have a developed faith and emotional countenance, don't punish him for being young. Christians, and particularly Christian parents, often develop a bad habit of implementing rules and expecting all families to implement the same rules for their kids. But not all families operate the same, and different kids need different levels of parental involvement. Be discerning with your child and have a little faith in him. If his life bears fruit and his behavior is consistent with his words, you may not have to monitor him as much. In other words, let your teen be innocent until proven guilty, not the other way around.

On the other hand, if your teens are being as sharp as a bag of hair and acting like a slut, ruffian, or gangbanger, deal with them swiftly and powerfully. You may have to implement all the strategies we've mentioned and monitor the computer all the time. Remember, your house is not a democracy. Some teens test every square inch of your patience, and when they try to be rebellious, you have to put them in their place. As Bill Cosby jokingly says, "I brought you into this world, and I'll take you out of it!"

Your number one priority is to guard your children's hearts. As Scripture wisely notes, "Above all else, guard your heart, for it is the wellspring of life" (Proverbs 4:23). Kids are not equipped to guard their own hearts, and we have to help them until they are mature enough to leave the nest. Regardless of how strong their wings are, if their hearts are damaged, they will not be able to soar the way God intended them to. Our responsibility is to protect them, nurture them, grow them, and at the right time, push them out of the nest so they become eagles themselves.

〈〈 〉〉

Most parents are intimidated by the whole MySpace revolution. Originally, I thought it was because of the technology and the aversion to learning how to navigate the online community. The more

I've discussed it with parents, however, I've learned that many of them are not intimidated by the technology—they are intimidated by their children. Their kids are so much more skilled at navigating the pages and creating profiles that they feel they'll never be able to keep up. As with video games, many parents don't try simply because they don't want to look dumb in front of their kids.

But parenting is about looking dumb! Most teens go through a stage where they don't think their parents know anything and Mom and Dad are way uncool. If kids are going to think that anyway, what is stopping you from dropping your pride at the front door and diving headfirst into the virtual waters? Of course you are going to feel dumb the first time you try to navigate around. I felt dumb the first time I got online. I also felt dumb the first time I tried to ride a bike or drive a car. But the more times I did those things, the more skilled I became. The same can be said about navigating MySpace.

And truth be told, your kids probably don't know that much about MySpace. That is why some teens are getting in trouble. Yeah, they can create extraordinary-looking profiles and navigate like Magellan, but most kids have never taken the time to learn the basics the way you are doing right now. When you review their profile and ask them to make some changes, they are likely to respond, "Well, Mom, I don't think you can do that."

That is when you can ratchet up your coolness factor about ten notches. With your newfound knowledge, you can quickly respond, "Oh yeah, you can. Just go to your home page, click on Edit Profile, scroll down to Privacy Settings and click the right box. That should do it."

Then bask in your moment of glory.

6

My Life as a 16-Year-Old

A Behind-the-Scenes Look at the Life of an Online Teenager

Foolishness is bound up in the heart of a child.
PROVERBS 22:15 NASB

UP TO NOW, WE'VE TALKED a little bit about MySpace from an adult's perspective. But now we are going to examine it from a teen's perspective. Before I started writing this book, I took the liberty to create two fake accounts—one of a 16-year-old girl and one of a 16-year-old boy—and for a month, I did a little undercover investigation. I was surprised by what I found and by what I didn't find. But don't listen to me. Listen to my two much younger, cooler, and dare I say, better looking alter-egos, Susie Teenager, a.k.a. "Susie Q" (www.myspace.com/susieteenager), and Jonny Popular, a.k.a. "JP" (www.myspace.com/jonnypopular).

A lot of the investigations that groups such as *Dateline* have undertaken were designed to prove one thing—MySpace is dangerous. Instead of taking a real, honest, and open look at what teens deal with in online communities, they have focused solely on a few unfortunate incidents and the dangers of sexual predators. And in no way do I want to downplay the dangers that lurk online—the virtual world *can* be dangerous. But it doesn't have to be. More than 20 million teenagers surf MySpace every day, and the majority of them are good kids. Some are a little misguided, and many are a little too trusting, but they are good kids just trying to grow up in a crazy world.

The outcome of any experiment is only as good as the variables you use to set it up. If you want to show that teens are privy to drug-related conversations, set up a teen's profile to show that he supports marijuana use and have him join groups that talk about it. If you want to show that teens are vulnerable to inappropriate sexual behavior, entice other sexual deviants to her account with erotic pictures and flirty behavior. As the old adage suggest, "Birds of a feather flock together." Teens who are like-minded often stick together. The reason you don't want your son hanging out with gangbangers in the real world is that you don't want him involved in that type of behavior. The same logic applies to MySpace. But what would happen if teens stated that they are actually Christians? Would they still attract a rough crowd, or would their proclamation keep some troubles away? You are about to find out.

The Social Experiment

When I set up Susie Teenager's and Jonny Popular's accounts, I did it very strategically. First of all, I made both of them 16-year-olds so they were on a level playing field. If some challenges specifically applied to girls and not to boys, or vice versa, I wanted those to be revealed. I also tried to make them as cool and relevant as possible. I wanted them to be relatively good-looking teens to attract others, so I copied pictures of aspiring male and female models from other places on the Internet. On Susie's account, I said she likes movies such as *How to Lose a Guy in 10 Days,* she thinks Justin Timberlake is hot, and she likes watching *American Idol.* And her headline reads, "It's…well, ya know…all about me!" (If that doesn't shout teenager, I don't know what does.) On Jonny's account, I stated that he is an athlete who likes the television show *24* and *Monday Night Football.* He also likes the movie *Gladiator,* and his occupation is "professional air guitarist." His headline reads, "I'm just a boy, falling for a girl, which girl is yet to be determined…"

These were their stats at the end of the month:

Category	Susie Teenager	Jonny Popular
Profile Views	474	302
Number of Friends	52	41
Number of Friends of the Opposite Sex	49	37
Number of Friends Proactively Added	0	8
Number of E-mails Received	96	23
Number of Comments	20	35
Picture Comments	17	6

Setting up fake accounts is relatively easy if you have the time and understand the technology. So that no one could track me, I set up bogus e-mail addresses and then went through the prescribed process that we talked about earlier in the book to get on MySpace. I grabbed different pictures from around the Internet to show off their families and their dogs, and I made up all the information on their profiles. I also put them in different parts of the country to see if location made any difference to this dynamic generation. Susie is in Dallas, Texas, and Jonny is in Los Angeles, California. The setup process is very simple and virtually untrackable. The only thing I did to associate my true identity with Susie or Jonny was post a link to my latest book, *Undressed: The Naked Truth about Love, Sex, and Dating,* in each of their profiles. It wasn't just a shameless plug for my book—I was showing that they were both interested in relationships, and I was giving teens a relevant resource in case they were searching.

Most importantly, I stated that both Susie and Jonny were Christians. I didn't doctor their sites to make them look superconservative or ultra holy, but I did make it obvious that they were relatively good kids who loved the Lord. I wanted them to exemplify a sense of faith while still being relevant to the kids around them. And what I learned was very interesting…

Lessons from My Teenage Life

Most of us haven't been teenagers for quite a while, and we've forgotten what fighting hormones, acne, and peer pressure feels like. As adults, we can easily look at our children's lives and spot successful or self-destructive patterns because we have the blessing of hindsight; we've already been down that road. But for teens these challenges are new, and they are bombarded in many ways that we weren't when we were growing up.

This is no excuse for teens to act stupid, of course. It should be more of a reminder to parents that in order to raise a godly child, you are going to have to stick close to his side. Graphic television images, pornographic magazines, and shady Internet sites are just a few of the stumbling blocks that teens will trip over if you don't guide them on their way. And those are the obvious ones. The more dangerous and less noticeable landmines are the habits they pick up from those they trust the most—their friends and family. In other words, if you want your children to walk the straight and narrow, you are going to have to model that walk yourself.

Disguising myself as a teenager and wandering the streets of MySpace was a very eye-opening experience. I hope the lessons I learned as Susie Q and JP can help you better relate to your online teen.

Girls Are Verbal, Guys Are Visual

I quickly learned that attracting "friends" is much easier if you are a pretty girl than if you are a handsome guy. When I first started this experiment, I decided I was not going to proactively ask people to be my friends on either Jonny's or Susie's site. I was just going to unconditionally accept whoever came to my profiles. And at first, this seemed like a great plan. That is, until Susie had more than 25 friends and 100 hits on her account, and Jonny had 0 friends and

2 hits on his account. Guys obviously browse MySpace for physical beauty more than girls do.

I've been speaking on romantic relationships for more than ten years, and one of the principles that seems to hold true among all age groups is that "girls are verbal, guys are visual." In other words, girls feel more fulfilled when they are emotionally connected with another person, usually through heartfelt conversation, and guys feel more fulfilled when they are physically connected, usually through stimulating visual images. In MySpace, teenage girls are more likely to spend time with someone online who is willing to have a deep, intimate, personal conversation with them. Girls usually don't prefer to have lots and lots of acquaintances. They like to have a smaller, close-knit group of friends with whom they can share their feelings and thoughts.

On the other hand, guys are visual creatures. The most visited profiles on MySpace are of porn stars such as Tila Tequila and Jenna Jamison. Guys place a higher value on aesthetic beauty than girls do, and if you view many teenage guys' Top 8, you'll see a number of physically beautiful women. The reason Susie Q gathered friends more quickly than JP is because she is an attractive girl, and many guys rank that as a deciding factor for friendship. Only when I broke my initial rules with JP and had him ask a few girls to be his friends did I receive more friend requests for him. Other teenage girls decided to become JP's friends because they noticed sweet comments I had left on other girls' sites. They were intrigued by what he said.

What does all this mean? It means that teenage girls are more likely to be enticed by online predators who try to fill an empty emotional need, and teenage boys are more likely to be enticed by girls who can fulfill a physical desire. Teen girls are usually more at risk of taking an online relationship into the real world. Most of the problems that the media have highlighted involve young girls who met older guys on MySpace and agreed to rendezvous in the bricks-and-mortar world.

But I learned that these connections don't just magically happen. Predators use bait, and they look for tendencies in a girl's profile that may make her more susceptible to a come-on. Girls who talk about loving to party, loving to have sex, and loving to be wild are more likely to be approached by strange men. Because of Susie Q's more conservative profile, she only got a few unsolicited off-color comments, and in comparison to many of the things I've seen online, they really weren't that bad. Still, be prepared...the rest of this section includes some language you hope you never see on your kids' sites!

> So what up Susie my name is Kenny but a lot of people call me hotboy because am so sexy so write me back so can get to know more about you
>
> KENNY

> Damn girl are you a model? All those pics. of you are fine as hell...I bet you got all the guys in your school rap around your finger!! Well anyways if ya want a new friend add me!!
>
> RYAN

> so thx for the comment btw your pretty freakin hooootttt just thought i ould let you kno that
>
> JEREMY

> damn gurl looking good
>
> JOHN

Only when Susie Q became a little frisky and reposted an e-mail bulletin that was being passed around did a couple comments get spicy. One of the e-mails that was forwarded around read, "If you had me alone...locked up iin your room for twenty-four hours &

we could do whatever you wanted what would you do with me?"
(This is the kind of stuff some teenagers pass around.)

> Well the lights would be dim...and music would be playing
> soft and slow...and we would be under the covers...and
> then...i would slowly feel your body against mine....then
> i start kissing you at the neck...slowly going down your
> chest and stomach...going down even farther...using my
> tongue to give you divine pleasure...then i would make my
> way back up and let our tongues play with each other...
> next i would pick you up and firmly but softly slam you
> against the wall and hold your hands above your head
> while you fall into a place you never dream of...and this
> would go on for a few hours...give or take a sec...but yeah
> it would be something along those lines...and you ask and
> i told!! i wouldn't really have you doing anything...i would
> be doing everything and that how i do it!!
>
> RYAN

After I read this, of course, I wanted to hunt this 17-year-old
Plano, Texas, punk down and give him the beating of a lifetime.
But I should have expected this kind of talk from a kid who has a
Corona, handcuffs, and a "Wanted: Many Sexual Positions Available" poster on his site. No matter how many times you hear a kid
correspond inappropriately, knowing that teens talk this way is still
disturbing, especially since many of them don't even know what they
are saying. However, you are bound to have some of this in a community of 20 million teens, especially when you entice them with
a suggestive bulletin. Even though Susie was obviously a Christian,
some guys still wanted to be frisky simply because she was cute.

On the other hand, Jonny attracted girls who didn't seem to
be as interested in a sexual relationship but seemed to be much
more interested in a spiritual or emotional one. Teenage boys rarely
express their beliefs, and because of this, I think Jonny attracted a
relatively good group of girls. Few wild women were in his group,
and of the ones that were, the majority were proactively invited
by Jonny to be his friends. Although his profile was not any more

overtly Christian than Susie Q's, he seemed to naturally keep the troublemakers away.

> ok, i see. thats great! I do try to read but lately i havent been able to. But I have been wanting to finish reading Romans. Gosh, its been awhile since I've talked to someone whose really excited about God.
>
> KEREN

> hey I just found you on Christian teens myspace group and thought I'd add you? If you aren't into adding strangers thats cool too! God Bless
>
> BRITTANY

There were only a couple girls who got a little mischievious in our conversations, and in order to get them to open up, JP had to e-mail them multiple times.

> Actually, theres only one person who knows everything about me, and thats how i added you, through her page. i mean...ive done crazy sh*t like bungee jump when i was drunk, and slpet in my car because i couldnt go home and just stupid sh*t like that, and also i did the sex thang, but im young so im not focused on it, ya know? they know i lie to them about sh*t, but if they knew what i ACTUALLY did instead of 'going to the movies' then theyd absolutely KILL me.
>
> PATTI

Teenage girls and guys are aware of their sex appeal and flirt—sometimes inconspicuously with oxoxoxox (hugs and kisses) and sometimes very blatantly (with erotic messages)—with one another on MySpace. Guys show love to get sex—girls show their sexiness to get love. As you can imagine, this can create a very dangerous, downward spiral for teens if it is not held in check. Girls want to be noticed, so they post more and more provocative pictures to get guys' attention. Guys continue to confirm their beauty by saying nice and sweet things on their accounts. It just goes around and around and around.

But when teens are open about their Christian beliefs, they are far less susceptible to problems, and the issues they do face are less severe. After listening to the media, I was anticipating that I would have to beat older men off with a stick on Susie's account and shield Jonny's account from naked women throwing themselves at him. Neither situation transpired. But we should note that teen girls can be lured away by seductive talk and teen guys can be lured away by seductive pictures. These things just seem to happen far less when the teen is firmly planted in Christ.

Girls Want to Be Sexy, Guys Want to Be Macho

Parry Aftab, the president of WiredSafety.org, the world's largest online safety and help group, says that many teens treat online communities like "attention competitions." They often engage in inappropriate conversations and show provocative pictures because they want others to notice them. A teen may do this for numerous reasons such as a shortage of attention from his parents, a lack of direction in his life, or a lack of self-confidence—but from a broader perspective, it all boils down to an unfulfilled relationship with Christ. Many kids feel a hole in their souls, and they are looking for a way to fill it. Through online communities like MySpace, teens can express this emptiness and connect with others who also feel lost.

You can see this on the profiles of some adults who surf the pages of MySpace as well. When people don't have any clear direction in their lives, they are far more likely to flaunt their boobs and their brawn. It is a cover for a lack of meaning and purpose. I heard the shouts of loneliness on a number of profiles while surfing MySpace both as Susie Q and as JP.

One of the girls that Jonny became friends with was Carla, better known as Gurl Gone Wild. Carla's background is pink Playboy bunnies. I think you know where this is heading. Even though this 19-year-old doesn't have pictures that are overly sexual, she does have pictures of her holding a beer, and she states in her About Me section that she likes to party. She also says that she would like to meet someone she can date if he isn't too far away. Jonny worked his way into the number one spot in her Top 8 friends list just by sending her a few flirtatious comments. When Jonny flirted with her, she wrote back, "yeah my voice is pretty just like my body is. so tell me a little about ur self young stud. ur body is also HOT."

The majority of guys who were friends with Susie Q talked about sports and girls on their sites. That was how they defined themselves. Most of the guys filled their top friend spots with beautiful women. On King of all Kings' site, ten of his top twelve were attractive women. On Robert's site, twenty of his top twenty-four were pretty girls. On Jarvis' site, eighteen of his top twenty are women. And the list goes on and on. The unspoken code among teen boys seems to be, he who has the most beautiful women as friends, wins.

Social interaction can be a good and healthy thing for teens, even on the Internet. But the wrong type of interaction will certainly be detrimental. Some teens are communicating well; many are doing it poorly. The fact that many girls are trying to be overly sexy and guys are trying to be uberly macho is evidence. Opponents of MySpace argue that teens should not practice their social skills on the Internet. Their contact should be limited to face-to-face and verbal interactions until they establish their own identity. But we do our children a disservice if we ignore the fact that the virtual world will play a big part in their lives. The answer is not to isolate them from online activities but to monitor them so that you can be part of the growth process. Curiosity may have killed the cat, but it doesn't have to kill the heart of your teenagers. You just need to be part of their development so they don't go to macho or sexy extremes.

Teens' Lingo

If you want to relate to your teenagers, you need to speak their language. This may sound easy, but let me assure you that the lingo has completely changed. Things can easily get lost in translation, especially on the Internet. When I first started conversing with teenagers and answering questions, I felt as if I needed a Captain Crunch secret decoder ring to figure out what they were talking about.

Kids toss around thousands of abbreviations and slang terms on MySpace. Some are easy to decipher, and others are virtually impossible to figure out. Some popular ones hide offensive language. For a more complete listing, check out online dictionaries of slang and abbreviations at websites like www.noslang.com. Here are a few of the more popular ones:

Netspeak

What Teens Write	What It Means
<3	love
18r	later
asl	age/sex/location?
bf/gf	boyfriend/girlfriend
bff	best friends forever
bfn	bye for now
brb	be right back
btw	by the way
cya	see ya
dk	don't know
f2f	face to face
g2g	got to go
gn	good night
gr8	great
idk	I don't know
jk	just kidding

jmo	just my opinion
lol	laugh out loud
myob	mind your own business
np	no problem
omg	oh, my God!
oxoxox	hugs and kisses
pls	please
ppl	people
qt	cutie
rotfl	rolling on the floor laughing
r u there?	are you there?
thx	thanks
toy	thinking of you
ttyl	talk to you later
wtg	way to go!

For the most part, I don't have a problem with teens using clever abbreviations to speed up their conversations. But parents need to make sure that their kids don't get so sloppy with their grammar that they are unable to write properly. Typeset slang works well for informal Internet conversations, but it should not be carried over into school or work or used to disguise inappropriate language.

Btw this iz jmo…idk exactly how ur kid will talk. Lol…

MySpace Is a Gap Filler

Most of the time, teens don't really talk about anything significant in their e-mail or comment correspondance. My friends and I often joke that MySpace is the best time waster ever designed, but we may have underestimated the accuracy of this comment as it pertains to teens. I received more than ten pages of e-mail on Susie's account, and the majority said things like this (I put my commentary in parenthesis for a little comic relief):

> Speedy—>chapin wrote, "hi im writing u just to see how r u ok bye."

(He must be on medication…)

> Gerardo wrote, "wuz up susie q.?? haha na but wat r u doing??"

(Was that English?! Can I get a translator in here?)

> Robert wrote, "hey i just wanted to say hi okay hi"

(This project isn't worth my time…)

> Oscar wrote, "hey I'm oscar and u?"

(No kidding…I wouldn't have guessed that since your name is on the e-mail!)

> Chewy!!! wrote, "thats cool, u seem like a cool girl so i fort i'de say hi, u neva can have 2 many friends now can u lol! x"

(Please tell me he doesn't want to be a writer when he grows up.)

For kids, MySpace is more of a way of saying, "Hey, I was thinking about you," than relaying important information. It is also a way of making new friends and sharing experiences. Adults sometimes struggle to relate to this desire because most of us already have more relationships than we are able to nurture successfully. Many of us don't want more friends—we just want to be able to spend time with the ones we have! Kids aren't at this stage yet. They are still trying to determine who their close friends are going to be, and MySpace is a way of exploring their options. Remember, most kids desperately want to be part of something, and for those who don't naturally fit into their class, school, or neighborhood, MySpace is a place to belong.

On Jonny's account, I received some even deeper, thought provoking e-mail:

> IM*-"SW33T"AND*-SOUR wrote, "hey cutie how is it going. So wats new in your life now days."

(If I get one more "What's Up?" e-mail, I'm going to go postal!)

> Keren wrote, "hey. . just bored and i wanted to say hey."

(Hey, back at you...)

> Briana wrote, "im just wondering but how come u want to be my friend?"

(What is this, twenty questions?!)

Participating in much of the mindless banter taking place on both Jonny's and Susie's accounts was extremely time consuming. But when I started talking about spiritual issues, teens opened up a little bit more and wanted to talk about things like church and Bible studies. The great thing about the next generation is that they are not afraid to broach sensitive subjects, and almost no topic is out-of-bounds. If they have questions about Christ, they'll ask. If they have questions about sex, they'll ask. In a world full of worthless information, they are hungry for truth and won't stop until they are satisfied. As parents, we just need to make sure they are satisfied with the right things.

More than MySpace

MySpace is simply a tool for many teens to establish more personal relationships. Twentysomethings may be content with using MySpace to keep up with friends all over the country, but many teens want more than that. On both Jonny and Susie's accounts, I received multiple e-mails asking if I had instant messenger and wanted to chat in real time. Teens usually don't have the resources to fly all over the country to meet people, so if they don't sense an immediate benefit from chatting with someone, they quickly drop the conversation and move on.

On Susie's account, many of the guys that she met lived in the same general location—Dallas–Fort Worth. The evidence isn't conclusive, but it suggests that these guys weren't just interested in keeping the relationship online. Susie didn't receive any direct requests to meet in person, but she did receive a few comments that were probing about what she was doing during the weekend. Many of the guys were obviously interested in meeting her in person, and had she made the offer, I'm sure she could have set up a face-to-face meeting.

The girls that contacted Jonny were more geographically diverse and didn't seem as interested in getting together. As I mentioned before, they were more cautious about personal interaction and more interested in a somewhat deeper online conversation.

Interestingly, many teens were quite content with their close group of friends in their own community. Breaking into some teens' circle of friends wasn't as easy as I originally anticipated. Some would include me in their friend's list, but I was obviously an outsider to their daily activities. A few girls asked Jonny why he wanted to be friends with them, and a few guys were hesitant to add Susie as a friend. And believe it or not, one person on each account called Jonny or Susie a fake—they saw right through my facade (although I thought I did a pretty good job of faking it). On Jonny's account, Emily wrote, "That looks like a fake picture…all your pictures do…and you are not popular…you are gay…dont talk to me." Her response was a little harsh but very effective! Some kids are pretty Internet savvy, and they can spot a faker, even in the virtual world.

Research shows that teens spend almost a third of their day engaging with communication tools, much of it on the Internet. Seeing that many of these teens are doing so with friends in their own community was reassuring. I didn't see a bunch of parents floating around in the virtual pool, but I did run into some parents online and found clear evidence about which kids were being monitored and which ones weren't.

《《 》》

Even though I only spent a month in Susie's and Jonny's shoes, the experience was very eye opening for me. I've been speaking to teens for years, and as most parents know, the hardest thing to accomplish is to get your kids to share their struggles as well as their joys. Most parents want to be involved in their children's lives, but they have trouble relating to them. The beauty of MySpace is that it empowers teens to openly share their lives. For parents who are looking for ways to relate to their teens, this can be a huge open door. Wise parents won't spy on their kids like Big Brother, but they will use this innovative tool to cleverly monitor and build relationships.

If you take the time to surf MySpace for a while, you'll see that the teens who are causing the most trouble are the ones who are not being supervised by adults. Parents can give a myriad of excuses why they can't watch their kids, but they are just that—excuses. Parents have no greater opportunity to leave a legacy than by helping their children become discerning, godly men or women. Many of the Christian teens I bumped into online were good kids, trying to sift through all the noise and find their way in life. A good parent will see this and walk the path with them.

PART III:

Plan

Frequently Asked Questions

A Quick Reference Guide to Understanding MySpace

*Be one who manages his own household well, keeping
his children under control with all dignity.*

1 TIMOTHY 3:4 NASB

WHEN *DATELINE* DID AN INVESTIGATIVE study of MySpace, they followed
a police officer who assumed a fake identity and attempted to surf
the virtual community as a teenager. They then spoke to parents to
see if they really knew what their teens were doing online. Margaret
Sullivan, the mother of Shannon Sullivan, listened to the undercover police officer as he revealed that on certain MySpace accounts,
he "found scenes of binge drinking, apparent drug use, teens posing
in underwear, and other members simulating sex, and in some cases
even having it." Margaret said she was shocked.[1]

And there lies the problem. The issue isn't that they found scenes
of drinking, drug use, or sexually explicit conversation—talk to
almost any teen and you'll find that they face these types of temptations on almost a daily basis. The issue is that most parents are
shocked. Most parents are far too naive when it comes to understanding and connecting with their children. Some parents don't
see any smoke, so they assume there is no fire, and they don't tackle
the tough subjects with their kids. Other parents have a disturbing
gut feeling that something may be wrong, but they just sit back
and hope that it will work itself out. Neither approach is biblical,
and our teens are suffering because of parents' lack of attention

and guidance. MySpace isn't creating all these problems. It is just revealing the disturbing facts that we've been afraid to face for far too long.

When Paul wrote to his young understudy, Timothy, he reminded him that godly parents are those "who manage [their] own households well, keeping [their] children under control with all dignity" (1 Timothy 3:4). We don't often hear the word "manage" applied to our families, but it is appropriate in this context. Much like a corporate manager of a Fortune 500 company, we need to not only direct the people underneath us but also understand, actively participate in, and carefully monitor all their steps along the way. If we want our children to be top-performing employees in this job called life, we have to help them manage their lives until they are ready to manage their own.

Much like the rest of the Internet, MySpace can be a dangerous place for teens if they are left unsupervised. Most parents undoubtedly want to understand all aspects of their children's lives, but many are too busy or flustered to manage all the details. To help you with this, I've put together a brief list of frequently asked questions to help you navigate the treacherous waters.

What are the age requirements for MySpace?

 I understand that children under the age of 14 are not allowed to use MySpace, according to their website and company policy. But I've also heard that some children under 14 have joined the online community and are surfing with 30-year-olds. What safeguards has MySpace put in place, and how does the member process work?

Great question. It is clearly stated that children under the age of 14 are prohibited from using MySpace, and new members are required to enter their birth date when opening an account. But it is an honor code system, and children can certainly lie and say that they are older than 14. MySpace has an automated search engine and a dedicated team checking the accounts at all times, and they will certainly delete an account if they believe a child is too young. However, many older adults lie about their age as well, so you really can't be certain about anyone's age. Even with a hundred or so MySpace employees surfing the community, enforcing these age restrictions is pretty difficult. Regardless of what the MySpace executives think, parents need to decide when and if their children are ready to be on MySpace. If you feel 14 years old is too young, then monitor your kids' online activities and don't let them join until they are ready.

Can MySpace verify the actual ages of users?

Could MySapce create some type of personal verification system, such as a credit card check, to open an account? Wouldn't that enforce the age policy and protect users from predators and scam artists?

Currently, MySpace has no formal verification process in place. It is on the honor code system. Yes, they could create a verification system, but they would alienate a large portion of their users. Many teenagers, rock bands, and overseas clients don't have credit cards and aren't using MySpace for business. A verification system could weed out some problems, but it would also drive away a significant portion of their user base, a step they are not willing to take. I happen to agree with the MySpace executives on this point and appreciate their willingness to make the site free and easy to navigate. The responsibility for how the site is used should be on the end user, and in the case of teenagers, on the user's parents. If you don't think your teen is mature enough to use the site, don't let him or her until you have discussed it.

Is MySpace a good thing or bad thing?

As a Christian and as a speaker who interacts with the younger generation, do you think MySpace is a good thing? Do you think MySpace will last, or is it just a fad?

MySpace *can* be a good thing—depending on how it is used. Like cell phones, e-mail, instant messenger, or other communication tools, it is only as effective and powerful as the end user. I've seen accounts where Christians are sharing Scripture, creating Bible studies, and connecting with other believers; I've also seen soft-porn accounts where lost souls are screaming out for attention. MySpace is simply a tool. Its contents reflect the person using it. I really don't know whether MySpace will be king of the online communities for long, but I do know that if MySpace disappears, a bigger, stronger, and more powerful online community will take its place. Online communication is here to stay and will only get more interactive. We just need to make sure that it never completely replaces real, face-to-face, human conversation.

Is the Internet safer than MySpace?

 From all that I hear on the news, MySpace is a dangerous place for teens. I don't have trouble letting my teenager surf the Internet, but I think I'm going to restrict him from MySpace. What do you think?

Because of all the negative media that MySpace has received recently, we could easily assume that MySpace is more dangerous than the Internet—but it is not. In fact, a teen can find more trashy and disturbing sites that are pornographic, drug- or violence-related, and vulgar on the Internet in general than he will be able to find on MySpace in particular. The real problem with MySpace isn't that the content is worse than the Internet; the real problem is that MySpace is easier to navigate, and you can link a person to a particular lifestyle or addiction. MySpace makes the information more personal.

If we are trying to be discerning parents, we would be wise to not let our children surf either the Internet or MySpace without parental supervision. The families I know that have "open computer" policies, allowing the parents to peek over their children's shoulder at any time, are the most successful at monitoring their children. And as the teens get older and prove that they deserve more autonomy, the parents slowly allow them more and more Internet freedom.

Are there other ways to protect our kids?

 In addition to making our teen's account private and scrubbing it for all personal information, what else can we do to monitor his behavior? Can we install other filters or software programs?

Absolutely—you can install other software packages to help monitor and protect your kids, and I would highly suggest buying one of them. Personally, I have very little experience with some of these programs, but after researching a number of products, parents seem to rave about the same ones time and time again. One product, K9 Web Protection (www.k9webprotection.com), won the iParenting Media Award. K9 Web Protection is a free Web filter that gives parents control over their family's use of the Internet. K9 won the award because it enables parents to monitor and control what sites their children access, and it enables parents to block offensive or potentially dangerous sites, including MySpace. K9 is the only Web filtering product to receive this honor. Another program, SafeEyes (www.safebrowse. com), was chosen as the number one Internet filter by *PC* magazine. SafeEyes can limit the time your teen spends online, block peer-to-peer file sharing, block any Internet application, control words on search engines, and log instant messenger chats. With SafeEyes, a parent can read a log of all the people your teens are talking to online and what sites they have visited. A third program, eBlaster (www.eblaster.com), was talked about on ABC's *20/20*. eBlaster can automatically forward a copy of every instant message, e-mail, chat conversation, or website that your teens access. With only a slight delay, parents can see everything their children are doing online. I would highly recommend getting one of these programs or a software filter similar to these to help monitor your children.

Are online safety and help groups available?

 I'm not a very savvy Internet parent. I'm sure I can get someone to help me load some software to my computer, but are other resources available to help keep me up to speed?

A few sites that you probably ought to remember include Wiredsafety.org, Blogsafety.com, and familywatchdog.us. Wiredsafety.org is the world's largest safety and help group. MySpace works alongside this advocacy group and often implements its recommendations, which include a set of safety tips that are available at the bottom of every MySpace page under Safety Tips. Blogsafety.com is a forum where parents and experts can talk about safe blogging and social networking. It also has tips and articles for parents to read and discuss. And familywatchdog.us provides maps and locations of registered sex offenders and predators in your area. I've yet to plug in an address where I haven't been horrified by the number of offenders in the area.

What are bulletins?

 I recently asked my son what he was doing on MySpace, and he said he was sending out a bulletin. What are bulletins, and how do they work?

Each user's home page has a link on the bottom left-hand corner that allows users to read and send bulletins. In its simplest form, a bulletin is a mass e-mail that goes to everyone on a person's list of friends. If you have ten friends, ten people will get the e-mail. If you have 10,000 friends, 10,000 people will get the e-mail. But instead of showing up in a user's inbox, a bulletin shows up on a bulletin board and can be read at the user's convenience. And like most mass e-mails, bulletins usually contain inspirational stories, ridiculous questionnaires, and personal marketing material. I like to refer to bulletins as *splogs*—half spam, half blogs—and usually a complete waste of time. Most of the users I know don't spend much time sifting through bulletins. But from time to time, you will find a diamond in the rough.

Can I delete my teen's account?

I appreciate your balanced perspective on MySpace, but after reviewing the site, I'm still not comfortable with it. I don't think it is appropriate for my children, and I don't think my kids are ready to handle it. Can I delete their accounts on my own?

I appreciate and respect your informed decision. As I mention in various parts of this book, MySpace isn't for everyone, and parents like yourself have to decide what is best for your family.

So, can you delete your children's accounts on your own? Yes... and no. As of January 2007, no automated system is in place that allows parents to go online, review their children's accounts, and delete them. In order to delete an account, you have to log on as your teen with the proper e-mail address and password. If your teen will give you this information, follow these steps to erase his profile:

1. Log on as the user with the correct e-mail address and password. If you don't know your child's password, you can retrieve it by clicking the Forgot Password? link on the Member Login box of MySpace. The password will be sent to the e-mail address used to log on to MySpace.

2. Click Account Settings.

3. Click Cancel Account (the link is near the top of the Account Settings page).

4. You will now see the Cancel Confirmation page. Click the red Cancel My Account button. You will be asked to enter a reason for canceling MySpace. You may skip this if you wish. Click Cancel My Account. MySpace will send

a cancellation e-mail to the user's e-mail address. The e-mail will include a link to confirm the cancellation of the account.

Note: Allow up to 24 hours for delivery of the e-mail. If it doesn't arrive, check your Spam/Bulk mail folder. It may have been incorrectly routed to protect you from receiving junk mail.

If your teen will not give you his e-mail address and password, remember that complaining loudly will probably only aggravate the situation. I strongly encourage parents to keep their cool and communicate with their kids. A decision like this requires the cooperation of everyone involved.

If you are determined to erase the account and your teen is determined to keep the account, you can contact MySpace either by phone or e-mail, and they will help you delete the account. I know a handful of parents who had to take this route.

Why does some of the information in chapter 4, "Sherlock Homes," not perfectly coincide with your own account, Jason?

 After reading through chapter 4, I realized that there were slight discrepancies, such as in the blogs you had listed and the number of friends you had. Why is that?

Ah, good catch, my friend! I'm glad you noticed the small discrepancies. Whether you know it or not, you have stumbled upon the power of MySpace. The reason so many people are drawn to this vibrant online community is that it is constantly changing. Things rarely stay the same on anyone's page for very long. From the time I wrote this book to the time it was published, my profile continued to change. If you see some small changes in layout, information posted, or number of friends, then I too have continued to change and grow. The same will be true of your children's accounts. Once you think you have a handle on everything in their profiles, they will change them. This may seem frustrating, but it is a good reminder to be constantly involved in their lives instead of just dropping in on them from time to time.

Are there any interactive tools on MySpace that can help parents?

 I appreciate all your insight and direction, but are any tools available that can help us with MySpace on an ongoing basis?

You don't think I would just toss this book into your lap and call it a day, do you? I know that raising children in the Internet world can be a daunting task, so I've created a special MySpace website to supplement this book. The site is www.myspacemykids.com. This site will familiarize you with MySpace and teach you how to navigate the virtual waters. You will be able to watch a number of powerful online instructional videos that will bring you up to speed on social networking. It is a fantastic interactive tool and a must-have for all parents looking to better understand their kids!

To Protect and Connect

Every Parent's Dream

*I have fought the good fight, I have finished
the race, I have kept the faith.*
2 TIMOTHY 4:7

PARENTS DREAM TO UTTER THE words above when their kids have finally grown up and have moved out of the house. To fight the good fight for the safety of your teens and to help them keep the faith isn't just admirable; it is godly. And it is attainable for all parents who are willing to dive headfirst into their children's worlds.

We've talked a lot about making a profile private, scrubbing all personal information, downloading software filters, and various other ways to protect your kids from predators. But the most powerful defense against drug dealers and sexual offenders is *you!* Nothing can substitute for an actively involved and loving parent. In a perfect world, if 20 million teenagers were on MySpace, at least 20 million parents would be monitoring their behavior and working with them. If our kids can network with one another, shouldn't we do it all the more?

Without question, dangers *are* lurking in the dark corners of MySpace, and we must protect our kids from them. Now that you have a more thorough understanding of this online community, I hope you can make informed decisions on how to guard kids' hearts. Some teens show an amazing amount of maturity and can handle most of the things that pop up in the virtual world. Others have their brains out on loan and need to be tracked with a pair of police dogs. As a parent, it is your responsibility to determine what your teens can handle and implement the needed safeguards.

From my experience, kids are more likely to get in trouble if they possess three things: (1) idle hands, (2) an unexercised mind, and (3) an uncommitted heart. When kids have idle hands—when they have too much free time and too little to do—they are more likely to get involved in sexual or problematic situations. When teens have unexercised minds—when they have not discussed sensitive issues with their parents—they are more likely to succumb to temptation. And when children have uncommitted hearts—when they don't believe in Christ or possess a strong set of family values— they are more likely to experiment with whatever is presented to them. Even though you can't monitor every action and help with every decision, if you can watch these three areas, you will greatly minimize the chances that your kid will make a poor, life-altering decision.

MySpace isn't inherently evil—it is what you make of it. In many instances, MySpace isn't creating problems, it is simply revealing the problems that have been there all along. If your son is collecting half-naked women on his account, he has probably been surfing the Internet for porn for quite some time. If your daughter is sporting black makeup and posting gothic pictures on her profile, she has probably been battling with loneliness or self-esteem issues right under your nose. If you don't think your teens can handle the challenges of MySpace, don't let them join the community until they are. MySpace isn't for everyone.

But if you do let your teens join the community, leverage all the tools available and devise a way to monitor their behavior. Allow this virtual world to be a second pair of eyes and ears for you. Interact with and encourage your children whenever you can while still providing a healthy amount of freedom. The more you can teach them while they are in your care, the better equipped they will be when they leave the nest. Tomorrow's adults will certainly face online challenges. If they have been coached, guided, monitored, and prayed for in the past, they will be ready to handle the future.

Whatever you do, don't panic. And don't jump to uninformed conclusions about MySpace or your teen. Instead of making a fuss in the media or picketing company headquarters, Christians can quietly represent Christ by simply being better parents than everyone else. Christian families who can teach their teens how to navigate this online community in a healthy and productive way will shout volumes about our faith and our God.

Notes

Chapter 1—aWholeNewWorld.com

1. Bill Hewitt, "MySpace Nation: The Controversy," *People*, June 5, 2006, 113-20.

2. Josh Billings, *Josh Billings: His Sayings* (Temecula, CA: Reprint Services Corp., 1869).

3. "National Teen Driving Statistics," Rocky Mountain Insurance Information Association. Available online at www.rmiia.org/Auto/Teens/Teen_Driving_Statistics.htm.

4. Stephen Covey, *The Seven Habits of Highly Effective People* (New York: Free Press, 2004), 235.

Chapter 2—Friends and Fiends

1. Kevin Poulsen, "Scenes from the MySpace Backlash," *Wired News*, February 27, 2006. Available online at www.wired.com/news/politics/1,70254-0.html.

2. Ibid.

3. Hewitt, Bill. "MySpace Nation: The Controversy," *People*, June 5, 2006, 113.

4. Jenn Shreve, "MySpace Faces a Perp Problem," *Wired News*, April 18, 2006. Available on line at www.wired.com/news/culture/1,70675-0.html.

5. "Kansas School Shooting Plot Failed," *CBS News*, April 20, 2006. Available online at www.cbsnews.com/stories/2006/04/20/national/main1524759.shtml.

6. "Student Suspended for Content of MySpace Account," NBC10.com, May 8, 2006. Available online at www.nbc10.com/print/9179348/detail.html.

7. "High School Boozers Busted by Blogs," *CBS News*, February 8, 2006. Available online at www.cbsnews.com/stories/2006/02/08/tech/main1296738.shtml.

8. Poulsen, "Scenes from the MySpace Backlash."

9. Ibid.

10. Matt Katz, "MySpace Users: Worries Part of Generation Gap," *Courier News Online*. Available online at www.c-n.com/apps/pbcs.dll/article?AID=/20060515/NEWS/605150314.

11. Bob Sullivan, "MySpace: Too Little, Too Late?" *The Red Tape Chronicles,* June 21, 2006. Available online at redtape.msnbc.com/2006/06/myspace_too_lit.html.

Chapter 3—My House Is Not a Democracy

1. Hilary Hylton, "Another Suit in the MySpace Case?" *Time.com,* June 22, 2006. Available online at www.time.com/time/nation/article/0,8599,1207043,00.html.

2. "Michigan Teen Home Safe and Sound." *CBS News,* June 12, 2006. Available online at www.cbsnews.com/stories/2006/06/09/tech/main1697653.shtml.

3. Daniel Wood, "Why Mom Enlisted an Online Sleuth to Keep Tabs on Child," *The Christian Science Monitor,* June 21, 2006. Available online at www.csmonitor.com/2006/0621/p01s01-ussc.html?s=u.

Chapter 4—Sherlock Homes

1. Bill Hewitt, "MySpace Nation: The Controversy," *People,* June 5, 2006, 113-20.

2. "Teen Charged with Threatening School Official," *MSNBC.com,* June 6, 2006. Available online at www.msnbc.msn.com/id/13162846.

3. Cited in Janet Kornblum, "Teens Wear Their Hearts on Their Blog," *USA Today,* October 30, 2005.

4. Cited in D.A. Huffaker and S.L. Calvert, "Gender, Identity, and Language Use in Teenage Blogs," Journal of Computer-Mediated Communication, 10(2), article 1. Available online at jcmc.indiana.edu/vol10/issue2/huffaker.html.

5. From your Home page, select Account Settings. Next to Privacy Settings, select Change Settings. Check the boxes to make your settings, and click on Change Settings at the bottom of the page.

Chapter 7—Frequently Asked Questions

1. Rob Stafford, "Why Parents Must Mind MySpace," *Dateline NBC,* April 5, 2006. Available online at www.msnbc.msn.com/id/11064451/

About the Author

Jason Illian is considered one of the best and brightest young speakers and writers in America. Exhibiting a rare combination of personal humility and professional will, he inspires people to think and act in ways previously unimaginable. For the last decade, Jason has toured the United States, speaking on various issues affecting the younger generation, including premarital sex, faith, and online dangers. He has addressed teens in both schools and churches and is passionate about empowering the next generation of leaders. Charismatic and clever, Jason is a master storyteller with the gift for making the seemingly complex easy to understand. The oldest of three grown boys, Jason brings a hip yet educational approach that will help parents better understand their kids.

Graduating magna cum laude from Texas Christian University with a BBA in international finance, Jason continued his education by studying with TCU and the London School of Economics. In addition to being an NCAA academic all-American and captain of the TCU football team, Jason was named one of the top 20 students in America by *USA Today* and was a finalist for the Rhodes Scholarship. His first book, *Undressed: The Naked Truth About Love, Sex, and Dating* also addresses teen issues. This is his second book.

Other Good Harvest House Reading

THE 10 BEST DECISIONS EVERY PARENT CAN MAKE
Bill and Pam Farrel

With biblical insight and personal experience, the Farrels encourage you to make the ten most important decisions that will nurture and celebrate special needs, strong-willed, and prodigal children.

GOT TEENS?
Jill Savage and Pam Farrel

Jill Savage and Pam Farrel offer commonsense solutions, insightful research, and creative ideas to help you guide your children successfully into adulthood. You'll discover biblical advice, support, and encouragement for your journey.

HELPING YOUR KIDS DEAL WITH ANGER, FEAR, AND SADNESS
H. Norman Wright

Parents never like to see their child struggle, especially with dark emotions like anger, fear, and depression. Family counselor Norm Wright helps you understand these intense moods and develop sound principles to deal effectively with them.

THE POWER OF A PRAYING® PARENT
Stomie Omartian

The first book in Stormie Omartian's bestselling The Power of a Praying® series, now with a fresh cover, guides you in 30 simple chapters to effectively pray for your children's safety, faith, purity, and character.

WHEN GOOD KIDS MAKE BAD CHOICES
Elyse Fitzpatrick, James Newheiser, and Laura Hendrickson

Three qualified biblical counselors share how you can deal with the emotional trauma of when your child goes astray. A heartfelt and practical guide that includes excellent advice regarding medicines commonly prescribed to problem children.

WHEN YOUR TEEN IS STRUGGLING
Mark Gregston

For parents of teens who exhibit destructive or unhealthy behaviors and actions, Mark Gregston offers biblical guidance, encouraging stories, and a fresh message of hope as he shares the keys to turn struggle to success.

HARVEST HOUSE
PUBLISHERS

To read sample chapters of other books from
Harvest House Publishers, log on to our website:

www.harvesthousepublishers.com

HARVEST HOUSE PUBLISHERS

EUGENE, OREGON